THE

LOTTO PLANNER + *1990*

RESOURCE GUIDE

Compiled and Written by

Robert Serotic

With Special Thanks to James Burton, Timothy Campisi, Mark Garcia, Paul Kikeli, Julie Rodriggs and Matt Rossmeissl   **Third Printing**

Copyright ©1987, 1988, 1989 by Robert Serotic, San Francisco, California, USA
Design Copyright © 1988 by Campisi/Lundin Advertising, San Jose, California
Cover Design Copyright © 1988, 1989 by Georgeous Graphics, Los Altos, California,

EURO LOTTOGRAF™, SIX-GROUP SYSTEMS™, GROUPS SYSTEMS™, GIANTS™, PERMS™, SYSTANALYZER PC II-2™, JACKPOT TRAPS ™, DAILY PERMS™, CUSTOM WHEEL NETWORK™, LOTTERY DOLLARS™, and CONDITIONAL COMPOUND SYSTEMS™ are trademarks of L.S.I.Publishing, Inc.

Published by **L.S.I.Publishing, Inc.,**
1259 El Camino Real, Suite 217, Menlo Park, California 94025

Library of Congress Cat. in Publication Data Pending: Serotic. LOTTO PLANNER +
Third Edition, July 1989; 15,000 copies
Printed in the United States of America.

· ISBN   0-941271-40-4

NOTICE TO LAW ENFORCEMENT AND POSTAL OFFICIALS

L.S.I. Publishing, Inc. is a research and publishing company that provides reference materials to individuals interested in Lotto playing. This company does not offer lottery tickets for sale, nor does it participate in or conduct lotteries or games of chance. The company does not offer "Lucky Numbers" or participate in "Group Play."

CONTENTS

LOTTERY GAMES

The lottery has been placed among the most popular games for thousands of years. It is more popular than casino games or horse racing. It is indeed a game with an enormous following. Unlike its rivals, the lottery is a game for the masses. It is played by the rich and the poor, the educated and the less educated, and especially by those who would never enter a casino or a race track, even if there was one around the corner. Indeed, most lottery players are far removed from gambling and do not associate their involvement in the game with "immoral" conduct.

As proof, I can offer a study by L.S.I. Publishing of 3,000 lottery players. Lottery participants who consider the lottery as pure amusement totalled 85%, while 9% regard it as amusement with some risk, and only 6% of players see the lottery as gambling.

The conclusion is obvious. The lottery in today's modern world is not seen as gambling, since it is run by the government, the proceeds go to "noble" causes (education, social and cultural aid), and especially because it lacks that "momentous" instance of tension in betting which the player experiences in casinos or at the race track.

What makes a game of chance is the possibility of winning again, of raising the stakes and trying to win back one's losses *instantaneously*. This is the excitement, the joy and the disappointment of the gambler—control over one's self, assessment of one's possibilities and abilities. Players think that they can triumph over an electronic machine, and when in a couple of minutes they have poured their entire salary into it and don't get back a cent, they blame the machine for their failure as though it were a living creature who betrayed them.

During my studies in the casinos of Reno, Nevada, I observed the psychology of the Keno and slot machine player. I witnessed players talking to the mute machines as though to a friend. They coaxed it, soothed it, praised it, and then abused it in a most uncharitable manner. And there were also those who heartily cursed it the entire time.

And the race track? An amazing experience! The true fan of the horses looks on his favorites like they were his own children, and he is willing to bet his very last cent on them. And when they lose, and there is still some money left—here's always another chance. After all, in twenty minutes there is another race, another hope, another shot. And for most, another loss. But losing doesn't intimidate the gambler, for he will be back again tomorrow.

We do not see this type of behavior in the lottery. In particular, Lotto is one of the most calmest of games. With one or two drawings per week, you have four or six days to place a bet. And until the drawing takes place, you don't know whether you have won big or not. If you did not pick the winning numbers, you cannot attempt to immediately win again since the next drawing may be up to a week away. In the meantime, you can cool down, think things over, and hopefully decide to stay with the same $10 a week (or whatever your budget may be). For most people, Lotto lacks the impulsive element which would cause even the calmest casino player to lose his head (and control) and continue betting down to his last cent.

Lotto is a quiet game, far removed from gambling. And if the player has a well prepared plan for the game and a financial commitment which he never exceeds, then there is little threat. He will gain enjoyment from the game, and with a little luck, the hope for success. The lottery has produced tens of thousands of multi-millionaires around the world, while millions of others dream of becoming one of them. To have dreams is a wonderful thing, but to realize them is quite difficult. How many of your big dreams have failed to materialize? Sorry to say, probably most of them. One must always be a realist and set goals which can be reached. And the same is true of playing the lottery.

Most players play with the desire of winning the Jackpot. That is a fine goal. To win and to win big! But let's be honest. There are few whom this will happen to. On the other hand, how many will win second or third prizes? Tens of thousands. A second prize may pay anywhere from $1,000 all the way up to $10,000, which is no small sum. Now you can see that there are many opportunities to achieve success without winning a Jackpot. It is only necessary to know how to use these opportunities. Plan the game properly, do not raise your stakes, and hold on. Hold on and have faith. This is one of the principles leading to success.

You hopefully have learned how to play and use systems in my "Lotto—How to Play and Win" series of books. But if you want to learn again about the substitution of your numbers into my systems, you can use the SAMPLE TABLE. And my "Euro-LottoGraf" will be the best possible help to you in developing your own tickets. The "LOTTO PLANNER" will be the most helpful in planning your financial analysis, keeping records of your bets and wins, plus the numbers drawn and the prizes awarded in individual drawings. It will tell you what types of games we have in each present lottery state in the USA and in lottery countries abroad, along with the probabilities of winning in the various types of Lotto.

I will also show you how to play Lotto across the country and the world by presenting some of the best lottery subscription agencies here and abroad, including the popular Australian Lotto 6/45, the lotteries in West Germany and in Canada. I will also explain how you can join the world's largest Lotto club *LOTTO-ONE* with almost 4,000 players, which plays a full system for 22 numbers with 74,613 games in every Illinois 6/54 draw!

I am sure that the Lotto Planner+ will be a trusted advisor to you in the important process of winning the game. You too, hope to be a winner like the many millions of players around the world, and this publication can be a great help to you in reaching this goal.

LOTTERY STATES

When New Hampshire created the first lottery in the USA in 1964, no one paid much attention to this event. Exactly 20 years later, the lottery was legalized in California and four years after that the number of states with lotteries exceeded 33. From coast-to-coast, the passion for playing is so great that voters have approved the lottery in practically every state where it was proposed. Exceptions such as Nebraska, where the lottery was not approved, are rare.

The majority of states begin with an instant game (scratch-off tickets) and gradually move on to Pick 3, Pick 4 and the most popular Pick 6 Lotto (only Rhode Island, Illinois, New Jersey and Florida have Pick 5 Lotto). Recently, WIN 10 (in New York), similar to Keno, and Pick 7 (in Pennsylvania and Illinois) have also become very popular. Lotto is also played by citizens of non-lottery states; many ardent Lotto fans who cannot play "at home" often drive hundreds of miles to place a bet with their "neighbors." Thus, residents of Minnesota play in Iowa, players from Indiana hop the border into Illinois, and Arizona Lotto is popular among Lotto fans in Southern Utah. Even those who don't have a "Lotto Neighbor" play the Canadian, Australian, or even European lotteries through "mail subscription plans."

Throughout the USA, Lotto clubs are becoming very popular, mostly bringing together 4-8 players. This method of play makes it possible to employ more powerful and expensive Lotto Systems for a larger group of numbers, which individual players could not usually afford. Many clubs (as well as individuals) employ ultramodern computer technology, statistical software, combinatorial knowledge and the theory of probability to select their numbers. Lotto, originally a simple game of randomly selected "lucky" numbers, is fast becoming a hobby and daily amusement for many sophisticated players. Yes, LOTTOMANIA is here and no one can stop it! But why stop something which brings amusement and enjoyment to so many people, and rewards to the many "fortunate"?

In the following chapters, I shall alphabetically present all the states and their lotteries, the types of games, Lotto number wheeling systems and other details necessary to begin betting. At the end of the section will be a listing of countries and their lotteries which are accessible through Subscription Agencies. These agencies make it possible to play these games just by using your telephone and credit card. All of this information will be of help in deciding which type of lottery you want to play. Or perhaps you would rather like to bet while "on the road" if you are traveling to these countries sometime in the future.

It is very important to know in detail the individual state lotteries, since each state has a different type of game, different winning conditions, and different methods of paying prizes. In the USA, for example, there are 12 kinds of Lotto, many different types of "daily games" (Pick 3, 4, etc.), and dozens of "Instant Scratch Off" games. The following chapters will help you answer many questions concerning the individual lotteries, their games and the lottery industry.

Play With Control, Not Guesswork!   *Good Luck, Winners!*   **Robert**

ARIZONA STATE LOTTERY

✉ 4740 E. University
Phoenix • AZ 85034

☏ *office*   (602) 921-4400

Kind of Game	## Lotto 6/39 *The Pick*
Bet Slip	Five boards per bet slip.
Price per Ticket	$1 per single drawing.
How to Play	Select any 6 out of 39 numbers on one single board. A Pick Retailer will enter your play slip into the On-Line Terminal, which will print a ticket. Or, let the state lottery computer pick the numbers for a "Quick Pick" ticket.
Drawing	Saturday and Wednesday at 10 pm. Six numbers are drawn from a field of 39 numbers. A Bonus Number is drawn from the remaining 33 numbers.
Lotto Prize Pools	All players who have matched the winning numbers, in any order, share the prize money in that category:

Prize Category	Winning Numbers Guessed Correctly	Odds
Jackpot	(6 out of 6)	1:3,262,623
Second Prize	(any 5 out of 6+Bonus)	1:543,771
Third Prize	(any 5 out of 6)	1:16,993
Fourth Prize	(any 4 out of 6)	1:412

How the $ is Divided	*The Pick* is a pari-mutuel game and prizes are divided equally among winners in each prize category. From every dollar played, 47.3¢ is returned to players in the form of prizes.
Jackpot Payout	The Jackpot is guaranteed at $1,000,000 each drawing. The prize will be paid in 20 annual installments.
Multi-week Tickets	The same ticket may be played up to six drawings in advance.
How to Claim a Prize	**Under $100** — any Pick retailer will pay your prize; **Over $100** — any Pick retailer will give you a claim form to submit to the Arizona Lottery.
Collecting Prizes	Winners have 180 days from the date of the drawing.

•Other Lottery Games• •Pick-6 Lotto Wheeling Systems• •Computer Software for AZ• •Results Line—Winning Numbers•	Instant Scratch-Off Game ($1 per ticket) Go to pages 46-60 (Systems 1, 8) Go to pages 83-87 1-900-370-5112 ($.75 1st min, $.50 each additional min.)—go to page 89

CALIFORNIA STATE LOTTERY

✉ *Headquarters • Public Information Office:*
600 North 10th Street
P.O.Box 3028
Sacramento • CA 95812-3028

Ⓒ *office*   (916) 322-7415
    results   (916) 976-4CSL

Kind of Game	## Lotto 6/49 + Bonus Number
Bet Slip	Five boards per bet slip.
Price per Ticket	$1 per one single drawing.
How to Play	Select any 6 out of 49 numbers on one single board. A Lotto Retailer will enter your play slip into the On-Line Terminal, which will print a ticket. Or, let the state lottery computer pick the numbers for a "Quick Pick" ticket.
Drawing	Saturday and Wednesday at 7:57 pm. Six numbers are drawn from a field of 49 numbers. The Bonus Number is drawn from the remaining 43 numbers.
Lotto Prize Pools	All players who have matched the winning numbers, in any order, share the prize money in that category:

Prize Category	Winning Numbers Guessed Correctly	Odds
Jackpot	(6 out of 6)	1:13,983,816
Second Prize	(any 5 out of 6+Bonus)	1:2,330,636
Third Prize	(any 5 out of 6)	1:55,491
Fourth Prize	(any 4 out of 6)	1:1,032
Fifth Prize	(any 3 out of 6)	1:56

How the $ is Divided	California Lotto is a pari-mutuel game and prizes are divided equally among winners in each prize category. From every dollar played, 50¢ is returned to players in the form of prizes.
Jackpot Payout	Prizes over $1,000,000 are paid in installments over 20 years.
Multi-week Tickets	Play the same ticket up to eight drawings in advance.
How to Claim a Prize	**Under $100** — any Lotto retailer will pay your prize; **Over $100** — any Lotto retailer will give you a claim form to submit to the State Lottery.
Collecting Prizes	Winners have 180 days from the date of the drawing to collect.

•Other Lottery Games•	Instant Scratch-Off Game ($1 per ticket)
•Pick-6 Lotto Wheeling Systems•	Go to pages 46-60 (Systems 2,6)
•CA Subscription Agencies•	Go to pages 74, 75
•CA Lotto Pools and Clubs•	Go to page 78 (Lotto Power)
•Computer Software for CA•	Go to pages 83-87
•Results Line—Winning Numbers•	1-900-370-5112 ($.75 1st min, $.50 each additional min.)—go to page 89

COLORADO STATE LOTTERY

201 West 8th Street	Send *Entry* Tickets To	*office* (719) 546-2400
✉ Suite 600	**Weekly Drawing**	*results* (303)832-LUCK
P.O.Box 7	P.O. Box 4400	(719)542-LUCK
Pueblo • CO 81002-0007	Pueblo • CO 81010-4400	

Kind of Game

Lotto 6/42 *Pick 6*

Bet Slip

Five boards per bet slip.

Price per Ticket

$1 for each board played per single drawing.

How to Play

Select any 6 out of 42 numbers on each single board. The Lotto Retailer will enter your play slip into the On-Line Terminal, which will print a ticket with the selected numbers on it.

Drawing

Saturday at 9:58 p.m., televised statewide.

Lotto Prize Pools

All players who have matched the winning numbers, in any order, share the prize money in that category:

Prize Category	Winning Numbers Guessed Correctly	Odds
Grand Prize	(6 out of 6)	1:5,245,786
Second Prize	(any 5 out of 6)	1:24,285
Third Prize	(any 4 out of 6)	1:556
Fourth Prize	(any 3 out of 6)	1:37

How the $ is Divided

Colorado Lotto is a pari-mutuel game and prizes are divided equally among winners in each prize category. From every dollar played, 50¢ is returned to players in the form of prizes.

Grand Prize Payout

Grand prizes will be paid by a progressive annuity in 25 annual installments. In the case that the first payment is less than $10,000, the entire prize will be paid in a lump sum.

How to Claim a Prize

$150 or less — can be paid by Lotto retailer for 30 days after the drawing ;

$151 and more — any Lotto retailer will give you a claim form to submit to the State Lottery.

Collecting Prizes

Winners have 180 days from the date of the drawing to collect their prizes.

•Other Lottery Games•
•Pick-6 Lotto Wheeling Systems•
•Computer Software for CO•
•Results Line—Winning Numbers•

Instant Scratch-Off Game ($1 per ticket)
Go to pages 46-60 (Systems 16, 20)
Go to pages 83-87
1-900-370-5112 ($.75 1st min, $.50 each additional min.)—go to page 89

CONNECTICUT STATE LOTTERY

✉ 555 Russell Road
Newington • CT 06111

© *office* (203) 566-2912
results

| Kind of Game | **Lotto 6/40** |

| Bet Slip |
Five boards per bet slip.

| Price per Ticket |
$1 per single drawing.

| How to Play |
Select any 6 out of 40 numbers on one single board. A Lotto Retailer will enter your play slip into the On-Line Terminal, which will print a ticket. Or, ask for a "Quick Pick," and the on-line terminal will randomly generate a selection of 6 out of 40 numbers and print them on your ticket.

| Drawing |
Every Tuesday and Friday at 8 p.m., televised live on WTXX Channel 20.

| Lotto Prize Pools |
All players who have matched the winning numbers, in any order, share the prize money in that category:

Prize Category	Winning Numbers Guessed Correctly	Odds
Jackpot	(6 out of 6)	1:3,838,380
Second Prize	(any 5 out of 6)	1:18,816
Third Prize	(any 4 out of 6)	1:456
Fourth Prize ($3)	(any 3 out of 6)	1:32

| How the $ is Divided |
Lotto is a pari-mutuel game and prizes are divided equally among winners in the first three prize categories. There is a $3 fixed prize for matching 3 numbers. From every dollar played, 50¢ is returned to players in the form of prizes.

| Jackpot Payout |
The Jackpot is guaranteed at $1,000,000 each drawing. The prize will be paid in 20 annual installments.

| Multi-week Tickets |
Use an "Advance Action" bet slip and mark the appropriate box for 2, 5, 10, 26 ($25), 52($50) or 104 ($100) consecutive drawings. The agent will then print you an Advance Action Lotto ticket.

| How to Claim a Prize |
Under $600 — any Lotto retailer will pay your prize;
$600 and **over** — any Lotto retailer will give you a claim form to submit to the Lottery Headquarters.

| Collecting Prizes |
Winners have 180 days from the date of the drawing.

•Other Lottery Games•
•Pick-6 Lotto Wheeling Systems•
•Pick-3 and Play-4 Lotto Wheeling Systems•
•CT Subscription Agencies•
•Computer Software for CT•
•Results Line—Winning Numbers•

The Daily Numbers (Pick-3) • Play-4 • Instant
Go to pages 46-60 ((Systems 3, 10, 11, 17)
Go to pages 35-45
Go to page 74
Go to pages 83-87
1-900-370-5112 ($.75 1st min, $.50 each additional min.)—go to page 89

D.C. LOTTERY

✉ D.C. Lottery Board
2101 Martin Luther King, Jr. Ave, S.E.
5th Floor
Washington • D.C. 20020-5731

📞

office	(202) 433-8000
results	(202) 678-3333
Claim Center	(202) 638-1861

Kind of Game	## Lotto 6/36 *QUICK CASH*
Bet Slip	Five boards per bet slip.
Price per Ticket	$1 per single drawing.
How to Play	Select any 6 out of 36 numbers on one single board. A Lotto Retailer will enter your play slip into the On-Line Terminal, which will print a ticket. Or have the computer pick the numbers using a "Quick Pick" feature.
Drawing	Numbers are drawn daily (Monday-Saturday) at 7:58 p.m., live on WHMM-TV Channel 32.
Lotto Prize Pools	All players who have matched the winning numbers, in any order, share the prize money in that category:

Prize Category	Winning Numbers Guessed Correctly	Odds
Jackpot ($250,000)	(6 out of 6)	1:1,947,792
Second Prize ($1,000)	(any 5 out of 6)	1:10,821
Third Prize ($10)	(any 4 out of 6)	1:299

How the $ is Divided	*Quick Cash* is a not a pari-mutuel game. The prize payouts are fixed. From every dollar played, 50¢ is returned to players in the form of prizes.
How the Jackpot is Paid	A $250,000 cash prize will be awarded to each player who matches all six winning numbers. Match 5 of 6 winning numbers and win $1,000. Match 4 of 6 winning numbers and win $10. The full amount of the prize will be paid on each winning play, regardless of the number of winners!
Multi-week Tickets	The same ticket may be played up to six drawings in advance.
How to Claim a Prize	**Under** $100 — any Quick Cash retailer will pay your prize; **Over** $100 — any Quick Cash retailer will give you a claim form to submit to the State Lottery.
Collecting Prizes	Winners have 180 days from the date of the drawing.

•Other Lottery Games•

•Pick-6 Lotto Wheeling Systems•
•Pick-3, Pick-4 Lotto Perm Systems•
•Computer Software for DC•
•Results Line—Winning Numbers•

Daily Games—D.C. Lucky Numbers • D.C. 4 •
• Instant Game • **LOTTO AMERICA** (page 31)
Go to pages 46-60 (Systems 5, 9, 12, 24)
Go to pages 35-45
Go to pages 83-87
1-900-370-5112 ($.75 1st min, $.50 each additional min.)—go to page 89

DELAWARE STATE LOTTERY

✉ The Blue Hen Mall • Suite 202
Dover • DE 19901

℃ *office* (302) 736-5291

Kind of Game

Lotto 6/36

Bet Slip

Ten boards per bet slip.

Price per Ticket

$1 per two tickets per one single drawing.

How to Play

Select any 6 out of 36 numbers on one single board. A Delaware Number agent will enter your play slip into the On-Line Terminal, which will print a ticket. Or, ask for an "E-Z Pick," and the on-line terminal will randomly generate a selection of 6 out of 36 numbers and print them on your ticket.

Drawing

Every Tuesday and Friday at 7:28 p.m., televised live on WDPB TV 65 and WHYY TV 12.

Lotto Prize Pools

All players who have matched the winning numbers, in any order, share the prize money in that category:

Prize Category	Winning Numbers Guessed Correctly	Odds
Jackpot	(6 out of 6)	1:973,816
Second Prize	(any 5 out of 6)	1:5,411
Third Prize	(any 4 out of 6)	1:149

How the $ is Divided

Lotto is a pari-mutuel game and prizes are divided equally among winners in the first three prize categories. From every dollar played, 50¢ is returned to players in the form of prizes.

Jackpot Payout

The Jackpot is guaranteed at $1,000,000 each drawing. The prize will be paid in 20 annual installments. You can obtain claim information by calling the number above.

How to Claim a Prize

Under $600 — any Lotto retailer will pay your prize;
$600 and over — any Lotto retailer will give you a claim form to submit to the Lottery Commission.
Major prize claim centers will cash tickets up to **$5,000** each.
Brookside News Center • 53 Marrows Road • Newark
Johnny's Supermarket • 1200 Maryland Avenue • Wilmington
Lottery Office-Suite 202 • Blue Hen Mall • US 113 • Dover
Bodies Dairy Market • 222 Railroad Avenue • Millsboro

Collecting Prizes

Winners have one year from the date of the drawing to collect.

•Other Lottery Games•
•Pick-6 Lotto Wheeling Systems•
•Play-3 and Play-4 Lotto Wheeling Systems•
•Computer Software for DE•
•Results Line—Winning Numbers•

Play-3 (Pick-3) • Play-4 (Pick-4) • Instant
Go to pages 46-60 (Systems 5, 9, 12, 24)
Go to pages 35-45
Go to pages 83-87
1-900-370-5112 ($.75 1st min, $.50 each additional min.)—go to page 89

FLORIDA STATE LOTTERY

✉ Florida State Headquarters
Capitol Complex
250 Marriott Dr.
Tallahassee • FL 32399

℮ *office* (904) 487-7777
Claim information 900-407-CASH

| Kind of Game |

Lotto 6/49

| Bet Slip • Price |

Five boards per bet slip. $1 for two plays per one drawing.

| How to Play |

Select 6 out of 49 numbers on one single board. A retailer will enter your play slip into the On-Line Terminal, which will print a ticket.

| Drawing |

Every Saturday at about 10:58 p.m., televised statewide.

| Lotto Prize Pools |

All players who have matched the winning numbers, in any order, share the prize money in that category:

Prize Category	Winning Numbers Guessed Correctly	Odds
Grand Prize	(6 out of 6)	1:13,983,816
Second Prize	(any 5 out of 6)	1:55,491
Third Prize	(any 4 out of 6)	1:1,032
Fourth Prize	(any 3 out of 6)	1:56

| Kind of Game |

Lotto 5/39 *Fantasy 5*

| Bet Slip • Price |

Five boards per bet slip. $1 per one drawing.

| How to Play |

Select 5 out of 39 numbers on one single board. A retailer will enter your play slip into the On-Line Terminal, which will print a ticket.

| Drawing |

Every Tuesday and Friday at 11 p.m., televised statewide.

| Lotto Prize Pools |

All players who have matched the winning numbers, in any order, share the prize money in that category:

Prize Category	Winning Numbers Guessed Correctly	Odds
Grand Prize	(5 out of 5)	1:575,757
Second Prize	(any 4 out of 5)	1:3,387
Third Prize	(any 3 out of 5)	1:103

General Information (applies to both games)

| Grand Prize Payout |

Lotto 6/49—Grand Prize over $1,000,000 is paid in installments over 20 years. **Fantasy 5**—Grand Prize is paid lump-sum.

| Multi-week Tickets |

Lotto 6/49—play the same ticket up to 26 consecutive drawings.

| Claiming a Prize |

$599 or less—any retailer will pay your prize; Over $599—validate the ticket and file a claim form with any Lottery retailer.

| Collecting Prizes |

Winners have one year from the date of the drawing.

•Other Lottery Games•
•Pick-6 and Pick-5 Lotto Wheeling Systems•
•Cash-3 Lotto Perm Systems•
•FL Subscription Agencies•
•FL Lotto Pools and Clubs•
•Computer Software for FL•
•Results Line—Winning Numbers•

Cash-3 (Pick-3) • Instant Game
Go to pages 46-60, (Systems 2, 5, 6, 22)
Go to pages 35-41
Go to pages 69, 71, 74, 75
Go to pages 69, 78
Go to pages 83-87
1-900-370-5112 ($.75 1st min, $.50 each additional min.)—go to page 89

ILLINOIS STATE LOTTERY

✉ 201 E. Madison
Springfield • IL 62702

✆ office   (217) 524-5155
results *(in IL)*   1-800-252-1775
results *(a 50¢ fee)*   900-407-CASH

Kind of Game	## Lotto 6/54
Bet Slip • Price	Ten boards per bet slip. $1 for two plays per one drawing.
How to Play	Select 6 out of 54 numbers on one single board. A retailer will enter your play slip into the On-Line Terminal, which will print a ticket.
Drawing	Every Saturday evening, televised statewide.

All players who have matched the winning numbers, in any order, share the prize money in that category:

Prize Category	Winning Numbers Guessed Correctly	Odds (per 2 games)
Grand Prize	(6 out of 6)	1:12,913,583
Second Prize	(any 5 out of 6)	1:44,839
Third Prize	(any 4 out of 6)	1:763

Lotto Prize Pools

Kind of Game	## Lotto 5/35 *Little Lotto*
Bet Slip • Price	Five boards per bet slip. $1 per one drawing.
How to Play	Select 5 out of 35 numbers on one single board. A retailer will enter your play slip into the On-Line Terminal, which will print a ticket.
Drawing	Monday, Wednesday and Friday at 6:57 p.m., televised statewide.

All players who have matched the winning numbers, in any order, share the prize money in that category:

Prize Category	Winning Numbers Guessed Correctly	Odds
Grand Prize	(5 out of 5)	1:324,632
Second Prize	(any 4 out of 5)	1:2,164
Third Prize	(any 3 out of 5)	1:75

Lotto Prize Pools

General Information (applies to both games)

Grand Prize Payout

Call **1-800-252-1775**. **Lotto 6/54**—GP over $1,000,000 is paid in installments over 20 years. **Little Lotto**—GP is paid lump-sum.

Multi-week Tickets

Play the same ticket up to 15 consecutive drawings.
With the Lotto Subscription Plan—play 26, 52, or 104 drawings.

Claiming a Prize

$600 or less—any retailer will pay your prize; Over $600 or $600 or less claimed 90 days after the drawing—fill out a claim form.

Collecting Prizes

Winners have one year from the date of the drawing.

•Other Lottery Games•	Daily Games—Pick 3&Pick 4 • Instant Game
•Pick-6 and Pick-5 Lotto Wheeling Systems•	Go to pages 83-87 (Systems 5, 7, 18, 22)
•Pick-3, Pick-4 Lotto Perm Systems•	Go to pages 35-45
•IL Subscription Agencies•	Go to pages 74, 75
•IL Lotto Pools and Clubs•	Gold Lotto One; Gold Lotto Cash 5 (page 76, 77)
•Computer Software for IL•	Go to pages 83-87
•Results Line—Winning Numbers•	1-900-370-5112 ($.75 1st min, $.50 each additional min.)—go to page 89

IOWA STATE LOTTERY

✉ 2015 Grand Avenue
Des Moines • IA 50312

© *office* (515) 281-7900
results (Hotline) 800-542-0020
(only in Iowa)

Kind of Game	## Lotto 6/36 *Pick 6*
Bet Slip	Five boards per bet slip.
Price per Ticket	$1 per single drawing.
How to Play	Select any 6 out of 36 numbers on one single board. A Lotto Retailer will enter your play slip into the On-Line Terminal, which will print a ticket.
Drawing	Wednesday and Saturday at 6:28 p.m., televised statewide.
Wheeling System Play	Play 7 numbers instead of 6—7 different combinations for $7. Play 8 numbers instead of 6—28 different combinations for $28.
Lotto Prize Pools	All players who have matched all winning numbers, in any order, share the Jackpot. The remaining prize categories have fixed payouts:

Prize Category	Winning Numbers Guessed Correctly	Odds
Jackpot	(6 out of 6)	1:1,947,792
Second Prize ($500)	(any 5 out of 6)	1:10,821
Third Prize ($20)	(any 4 out of 6)	1:299
Fourth Prize (Free Play)	(any 3 out of 6)	1:299

How the $ is Divided	From every dollar played, 50¢ is returned to players in the form of prizes.
How the Jackpot is Paid	The prize is paid in a lump sum when the Jackpot is less than $100,000. If it is more than $100,000, the prize is paid in installments over a 20 year period.
Multi-week Tickets	The same ticket may be played for up to 10 or 52 drawings in advance.
How to Claim a Prize	**Under** $600 — any Pick retailer will pay your prize; $600 or **over**— any Pick retailer will give you a claim form to submit to the State Lottery.
Collecting Prizes	Winners have 90 days from the date of the drawing.

•Other Lottery Games•

•Pick-6 Lotto Wheeling Systems•
•Computer Software for IA•
•Results Line—Winning Numbers•

• Instant Game • Pull-Tabs •
• **LOTTO AMERICA** (page 31)
Go to pages 46-60 (Systems 5, 9, 12, 24)
Go to pages 83-87
1-900-370-5112 ($.75 1st min, $.50 each additional min.)—go to page 89

KANSAS STATE LOTTERY

✉ 128 N. Kansas
Topeka • KS 66603

☎ *office* (913) 296-5700

| Kind of Game | **Lotto 6/33** |

Bet Slip

Ten boards per bet slip.

Price per Ticket

$1 per two tickets per one single drawing.

How to Play

Select any 6 out of 33 numbers on one single board. A Lotto Retailer will enter your play slip into the On-Line Terminal, which will print a ticket.

Drawing

Wednesday and Saturday at 8:16 p.m., each drawing is held in a different city on a rotating basis.

Lotto Prize Pools

All players who have matched all winning numbers, in any order, share the prize money in that category:

Prize Category	Winning Numbers Guessed Correctly	Odds
Jackpot	(6 out of 6)	1:553,784
Second Prize	(any 5 out of 6)	1:3,418
Third Prize	(any 4 out of 6)	1:105

How the $ is Divided

From every dollar played, 45¢ is returned to players in the form of prizes.

How the Jackpot is Paid

The Jackpot is paid in a lump sum (guaranteed $25,000).

How to Claim a Prize

Under $600 — any Lotto retailer will pay your prize;
$600 or **over** — any Lotto retailer will give you a claim form to submit to the State Lottery.

Collecting Prizes

Winners have 365 days from the date of the drawing to collect their prizes.

•Other Lottery Games•

•Pick-6 Lotto Wheeling Systems•
•Computer Software for KS•
•Results Line—Winning Numbers•

• Instant Game•
• **LOTTO AMERICA** (page 31)
Go to pages 46-60 (System 4)
Go to pages 83-87
1-900-370-5112 ($.75 1st min, $.50 each additional min.)—go to page 89

MASSACHUSETTS STATE LOTTERY

✉ Main Office • Claim the Jackpot Prize
15 Rockdale Street
Braintree • MA 02184

☏ *office* (617) 849-5555

| Kind of Game |
| Bet Slip • Price |
| How to Play |
| Drawing |
| Lotto Prize Pools |

Lotto 6/46   *MASS MILLIONS*

Five boards per bet slip. $1 per one drawing.

Select 6 out of 46 numbers on one single board. A retailer will enter your play slip into the On-Line Terminal, which will print a ticket.

Friday at 7:55 p.m., televised statewide—WNEV-TV7.

All players who have matched all 6 winning numbers in any order share the Jackpot.

Prize Category	Winning Numbers Guessed Correctly	Odds
Jackpot Prize	(6 out of 6)	1:9,366,819
Second ($50,000)	(any 5 + Bonus #)	1:1,561,137
Third Prize ($5,000)	(any 5 out of 6)	1:39,028
Fourth Prize ($100)	(any 4 out of 6)	1:801
Fifth Prize ($2)	(any 3 out of 6)	1:47

| Kind of Game |
| Bet Slip • Price |
| How to Play |
| Drawing |
| Lotto Prize Pools |

Lotto 6/36   *Megabucks*

Five boards per bet slip. $1 per one drawing.

Select 6 out of 36 numbers on one single board. A retailer will enter your play slip into the On-Line Terminal, which will print a ticket.

Wednesday and Saturday at 9:55 p.m., televised—WNEV-TV7.

All players who have matched all 6 winning numbers in any order share the Jackpot.

Prize Category	Winning Numbers Guessed Correctly	Odds
Jackpot	(6 out of 6)	1:1,947,792
Second Prize ($400)	(any 5 out of 6)	1:10,822
Third Prize ($40)	(any 4 out of 6)	1:299
Fourth (Free Bet)	(any 3 out of 6)	1:24

General Information (applies to both games)

| How the $ is Divided |
| Jackpot Payout |
| Claiming a Prize |
| Collecting Prizes |

Both games are pari-mutuel games and the prizes are divided equally among winners. From every dollar played, 50¢ (6/36) and 60¢ (6/46) is returned to players in the form of prizes.

Paid in installments over a 20 year period. Claim at the main office.

$100 or less—any Lottery retailer will pay your prize; Over $100—a claim form must be submitted to the Lottery Commission.

One year from the date of the drawing. $2 prizes—30 days.

•Other Lottery Games•
•Pick-6 Lotto Wheeling Systems•
•Pick-4 Lotto Perm Systems•
•MA Subscription Agencies•
•Computer Software for MA•
•Results Line—Winning Numbers•

Daily Games—Pick 4 • Instant Game
Go to pages 46-60 (Systems 5, 9, 12, 13, 24)
Go to pages 42-45
Go to page 74
Go to pages 83-87
1-900-370-5112 ($.75 1st min, $.50 each additional min.)—go to page 89

MARYLAND STATE LOTTERY

✉ Maryland State Lottery
St. 204
Baltimore • MD 21215

📞 *office*   (517) 887-6800

Kind of Game

Lotto 6/44

Bet Slip

Five boards per bet slip.

Price per Ticket

$1 per one game (board) per single drawing.

How to Play

Select any 6 out of 44 numbers on one single board. Any Lotto Retailer will enter your play slip into the On-Line Terminal, which will print a ticket.

Drawing

Wednesday and Saturday at 7:55 p.m., televised statewide.

Lotto Prize Pools

All players who have matched the winning numbers, in any order, share the prize money in the Jackpot category. The remaining prize categories are fixed payouts:

Prize Category	Winning Numbers Guessed Correctly	Odds
Jackpot	(6 out of 6)	1:7,059,052
Second Prize ($600)	(any 5 out of 6)	1:30,961
Third Prize ($50)	(any 4 out of 6)	1:669
Third Prize ($5)	(any 3 out of 6)	1:42

How the $ is Divided

Lotto 6/44 is a pari-mutuel game and the Jackpot is divided equally among winners. From every dollar played, 50¢ is returned to players in the form of prizes.

Jackpot Payout

The prize is paid in installments over a 20 year period when the Jackpot per share equals or exceeds $15,000 per year after being annuitized.

Multi-week Tickets & Subscripton

Maryland residents can play 26, 52, or 104 drawings in a row. Pick up an application form from any Lottery agent.

How to Claim a Prize

$600 or less — any Lotto retailer will pay your prize;
Over $600 (except Jackpot) — any Lotto retailer will give you a claim form to submit to the State Lottery.

Collecting Prizes

Winners have 180 days from the date of the drawing.

•Other Lottery Games•
•Pick-6 Lotto Wheeling Systems•
•Pick-3, Pick-4 Lotto Perm Systems•
•MD Subscription Agencies•
•Computer Software for MD•
•Results Line—Winning Numbers•

Daily Games—Pick-3&Pick-4 • Instant Game
Go to pages 46-60 (Systems 14, 15, 19, 23)
Go to pages 35-45
Go to page 71
Go to pages 83-87
1-900-370-5112 ($.75 1st min, $.50 each additional min.)—go to page 89

MICHIGAN STATE LOTTERY

✉ Bureau of State Lottery
Box 30023
Lansing • MI 48909

📞 *office* (517) 887-6800

| Kind of Game | ## Lotto 6/44 |

| Bet Slip | Five boards per bet slip. |

| Price per Ticket | $1 per single drawing. |

| How to Play | Select any 6 out of 44 numbers on one single board. Any Lotto Retailer will enter your play slip into the On-Line Terminal, which will print a ticket. |

| Drawing | Wednesday and Saturday at 7:29 p.m., televised statewide. |

| Lotto Prize Pools | All players who have matched the winning numbers, in any order, share the prize money in that category: |

Prize Category	Winning Numbers Guessed Correctly	Odds
Jackpot	(6 out of 6)	1:7,059,052
Second Prize	(any 5 out of 6)	1:30,961
Third Prize	(any 4 out of 6)	1:669

How the $ is Divided

Lotto 6/44 is a pari-mutuel game and prizes are divided equally among winners in each prize category. From every dollar played, 45¢ is returned to players in the form of prizes.

Jackpot Payout

The prize is paid in installments over a 20 year period when the Jackpot per share equals or exceeds $50,000 per year.

Multi-week Tickets & Subscripton

Michigan residents can play 26, 52, or 104 drawings in a row. Pick up an application form from any Lottery agent and mail it completed with your check or money order to:
Subscription Unit • Box 30023 • Lansing • MI 48909
You will get a membership card indicating your starting date, number selected and number of drawing for which your membership is eligible.

How to Claim a Prize

$600 or less — any Lotto retailer will pay your prize;
Over $600 — any Lotto retailer will give you a claim form to submit to the State Lottery. Jackpot must be claimed at (517) 887-6840.

Collecting Prizes

Winners have 180 days from the date of the drawing.

•Other Lottery Games•
•Pick-6 Lotto Wheeling Systems•
•Daily-3, Daily-4 Lotto Perm Systems•
•Computer Software for MI•
•Results Line—Winning Numbers•

Daily Games—Daily- 3&Daily- 4 • Instant Game
Go to pages 46-60 (Systems 14, 15, 19, 23)
Go to pages 35-45
Go to pages 83-87
1-900-370-5112 ($.75 1st min, $.50 each additional min,)—go to page 89

MISSOURI STATE LOTTERY

✉ Missouri State Lottery
P.O. Box 1603
Jefferson City • MO 65102

📞 *office* (314) 751-4050

| Kind of Game | **Lotto 6/48** *Pick 6* |

Bet Slip — Ten boards per bet slip.

Price per Ticket — $1 per two games per one single drawing.

How to Play — Select any 6 out of 48 numbers on one single board. Any Lotto Retailer will enter your play slip into the On-Line Terminal, which will print a ticket.

Drawing — Wednesday and Saturday at 6:58 p.m., televised statewide.

Lotto Prize Pools — All players who have matched the winning numbers, in any order, share the prize money in that category:

Prize Category	Winning Numbers Guessed Correctly	Odds (per 2 games)
Jackpot	(6 out of 6)	1:6,135,756
Second Prize	(any 5 out of 6)	1:24,348
Third Prize	(any 4 out of 6)	1:475
Fourth ($1 Free Play)	(any 3 out of 6)	1:27

How the $ is Divided — *Lotto 6/48* is a pari-mutuel game and prizes are divided equally among winners in each prize category. From every dollar played, 50¢ is returned to players in the form of prizes.

Jackpot Payout — The Missouri Lotto Jackpot is a guaranteed minimum $1,000,000. The prize is paid in installments over a 20 year period.

How to Claim a Prize — $599 or less — any Lotto retailer will pay your prize; Over $600 — any Lotto retailer will give you a claim form to submit to the State Lottery (mailed or hand-delivered).

Collecting Prizes — Winners have 365 days from the date of the drawing. Players matching 3 out of 6 winning numbers must redeem their tickets within 30 days after the drawing.

•Other Lottery Games•

•Pick-6 Lotto Wheeling Systems•
•Pick-3 Lotto Perm Systems•
•MO Subscription Agencies•
•Computer Software for MO•
•Results Line—Winning Numbers•

Pick- 3 • Instant •
• **LOTTO AMERICA** (page 31)
Go to pages 46-60 (Systems 14, 15, 19, 23)
Go to pages 35-41
Go to page 71
Go to pages 83-87
1-900-370-5112 ($.75 1st min, $.50 each
additional min.)—go to page 89

NEW JERSEY STATE LOTTERY

✉ One Lawrence Park Complex
CN 041
Trenton • NJ 08625

✆ *office*   (609) 599-5800

Kind of Game

Bet Slip • Price

How to Play

Drawing

Lotto Prize Pools

Lotto 6/46

Five boards per bet slip. $1 per one drawing.

Select 6 out of 46 numbers on one single board. A retailer will enter your play slip into the On-Line Terminal, which will print a ticket.

Monday & Thursday at 8:58 pm, televised—Channel 23, 50, 52, 58.

All players who have matched the winning numbers, in any order, share the prize money in that category:

Prize Category	Winning Numbers Guessed Correctly	Odds
Jackpot	(6 out of 6)	1:9,366,819
Second Prize	(any 5 out of 6)	1:39,028
Third Prize	(any 4 out of 6)	1:801
Bonus Number	5 random digits	1:100,000

Kind of Game

Bet Slip • Price

How to Play

Drawing

Lotto Prize Pools

5 Card Lotto—Lotto 5/52

Two boards per bet slip—A and B. $1 per 3 games per one drawing.

Each Board consits of 3 games. For each game you must select any 5 of the 52 cards (02-10,J,Q,K,A; Hearts, Clubs, Diamonds or Spades).

Tuesday and Friday at 8:58 p.m., televised on Channels 23,50,52,58.

All players who have matched the winning cards, in any order, share the prize money in that category:

Prize Category	Winning Numbers Guessed Correctly	Odds
Cash Top Prize	all 5 winning cards	1:2,598,960
Second Prize	any 4 winning cards	1:11,059
Third Prize	any 3 winning cards	1:240

General Information (applies to both games)

How the $ is Divided

Grand Prize Payout

Claiming a Prize

Collecting Prizes

Both games are pari-mutuel games and the prizes are divided equally among winners. From every dollar played, 50¢ is returned to players in the form of prizes.

Lotto 6/46—the prize is paid lump-sum when the Jackpot is less than $150,000. Over $150,000—installments over a 20 year period.

$600 or less—any Lottery retailer will pay your prize; Over $600—a claim form must be submitted to the Lottery Commission.

Winners have one year from the date of the drawing.

•Other Lottery Games•
•Pick-6 and Pick-5 Lotto Wheeling Systems•
•Pick-3, Pick-4 Lotto Perm Systems•
•Computer Software for NJ•
•Results Line—Winning Numbers•

Daily Games—Pick 3&Pick 4 • Instant Game
Go to pages 46-60 (Systems 13, 22)
Go to pages 35-45
Go to pages 83-87
1-900-370-5112 ($.75 1st min, $.50 each additional min.)—go to page 89

NEW YORK STATE LOTTERY

✉ Swan Street Bldg. 1
Empire State Bldg.
Albany • NY 12223

℃ *office*
results

(518) 474-2037
(212) (718) (516)
(914) 976-2020

| Kind of Game |
| Bet Slip • Price |
| How to Play |
| Drawing |
| Lotto Prize Pools |

Lotto 6/54

Ten boards per bet slip. $1 per two games per one drawing.

Select 6 out of 54 numbers on one single board. A retailer will enter your play slip into the On-Line Terminal, which will print a ticket.

Wednesday and Saturday at 10:30 p.m., televised—WPIX TV-11.

All players who have matched all 6 winning numbers in any order share the prize money in that category:

Prize Category	Winning Numbers Guessed Correctly	Odds (per 2 games)
Jackpot	(6 out of 6)	1:12,913,583
Second	(any 5 out of 6)	1:44,839
Third Prize	(any 4 out of 6)	1:763
Fourth Prize	(any 3 out of 6 + Suppl.)	1:597

| How the $ is Divided |

New York's Lotto 6/54 is a pari-mutuel game and the prizes are divided equally among winners in each prize category. From every dollar played, 40¢ is returned to players in the form of prizes (less 2¢ taken out for a reserve fund).

| Jackpot Payout |

About two weeks after a Jackpot winning is claimed, the winner is presented with a check which represents one twenty-first (1/21) of the total Jackpot. Beginning the following year, the winner receives 20 equal payments. These payments include the interest from the investment.

| Kind of Game |
| Bet Slip • Price |
| How to Play |
| Drawing |
| Lotto Prize Pools |

Lotto 6/40   *CASH 40*

Ten boards per bet slip. $1 per two games per one drawing.

Select 6 out of 40 numbers on one single board. A retailer will enter your play slip into the On-Line Terminal, which will print a ticket.

Monday at 10:30 p.m., televised—WPIX-TV11.

All players who have matched all 6 winning numbers in any order share the prize money in that category:

Prize Category	Winning Numbers Guessed Correctly	Odds (per 2 games)
Jackpot	(6 out of 6)	1:1,919,190
Second Prize	(any 5 out of 6)	1:9,407
Third Prize	(any 4 out of 6)	1:228

| How the $ is Divided |

Cash 40 is a pari-mutuel game and the prizes are divided equally among winners in each prize category. From every dollar played, 40¢ is returned to players in the form of prizes (less 2¢ taken out for a reserve fund).

| Jackpot Payout |

Jackpot is paid in one single payment—cash.

NEW YORK STATE LOTTERY

Kind of Game	**KENO** *WIN 10*

Bet Slip • Price

Five boards per bet slip. $1 per one drawing.

How to Play

You may choose 3, 4, 5, 6, 7, 8, 9, or 10 numbers between 1 and 80. Each choice represents the type of game you play:

Pick 3	play 3 numbers on one single board
Pick 4	play 4 numbers on one single board
Pick 5	play 5 numbers on one single board
Pick 6	play 6 numbers on one single board
Pick 7	play 7 numbers on one single board
Pick 8	play 8 numbers on one single board
Pick 9	play 9 numbers on one single board
Pick 10	play 10 numbers in one single board

A Lotto retailer will enter your bet slips into the On-Line Terminal and print a *KENO* ticket.

Drawing

Every day 20 numbers are drawn from a field of 80 numbers.

Lotto Prize Pools

You can match the winning numbers in any order. If you select 6 or more numbers, you then have more than one way to win. The following chart shows the KENO prize levels, prize amounts, and chances of winning:

Type Of Bet	Winning Numbers Guessed Correctly	Prizes	Odds
PICK 3	(3 out of 3)	$25	1:72
PICK 4	(4 out of 4)	$100	1:326
PICK 5	(5 out of 5)	$500	1:1,551
PICK 6	(6 out of 6)	$1,500	1:7,753
	(5 out of 6)	$50	1:323
PICK 7	(7 out of 7)	$7,500	1:40,979
	(6 out of 7)	$250	1:1,366
PICK 8	(8 out of 8)	$25,000	1:230,115
	(7 out of 8)	$1,500	1:6,232
PICK 9	(9 out of 9)	$100,000	1:1,380,688
	(8 out of 9)	$3,000	1:30,682
	(7 out of 9)	$250	1:1,690
PICK 9	(10 out of 10)	JACKPOT	1:8,911,711
	(9 out of 10)	$6,000	1:163,381
	(8 out of 10)	$300	1:7,384
	(7 out of 10)	$25	1:621
	(0 out of 10)	$4	1:22

General Information (applies to all three games)

Claiming a Prize

$600 or less—any Lottery retailer will pay your prize; Over $600—a claim form must be submitted to the Lottery Commission.

Collecting Prizes

Winners have one year from the date of the draw to claim the prizes.

•Other Lottery Games•
•Pick-6 Lotto & KENO Wheeling Systems•
•Daily Number&Win-4 Lotto Perm Systems•
•NY Subscription Agencies•
•Computer Software for NY•
•Results Line—Winning Numbers•

Daily Games—The Daily Number&Win-4 • Instant
Go to pages 46-60 (Systems 3, 7, 10, 11, 17, 18)
Go to pages 35-45
Go to pages 71, 74, 75
Go to pages 83-87
1-900-370-5112 ($.75 lst min, $.50 each additional min.)—go to page 89

OHIO STATE LOTTERY

✉ 615 West Superior Avenue
Cleveland • OH 44113

℃ *office* (216) 622-3200
results 1-900-260-1234

Kind of Game

Lotto 6/44 *SUPER LOTTO* & The Kicker

Bet Slip • Price

Ten boards per bet slip. $1 per single drawing.

How to Play

Select any 6 out of 44 numbers on one single board. Any Lotto Retailer will enter your play slip into the On-Line Terminal, which will print a ticket.

Drawing

Wednesday and Saturday at 7:29 p.m., televised statewide.

Lotto Prize Pools

All players who have matched all winning numbers, in any order, share the Jackpot equally. The remaining prize categories have fixed payouts:

Prize Category	Winning Numbers Guessed Correctly	Odds
Jackpot	(6 out of 6)	1:7,059,052
Second Prize ($1,000)	(any 5 out of 6)	1:30,961
Third Prize ($75)	(any 4 out of 6)	1:669

How the $ is Divided

From every dollar played, 45¢ is returned in the form of prizes.

Jackpot Payout

The prize is paid in installments over a 20 year period when the Jackpot per share equals or exceeds $250,000 per year.

How to Claim a Prize

$599 or less — any Lotto retailer will pay your prize;
Over $599 — Third Prize winners of more than $599 and the Second Prize winners must file a claim with a lottery sales agent (a check will be mailed). Or, a Quick Cash option—immediate bank payment —can be used. Both processes require validation by an agent.
Jackpot winners must contact the nearest Ohio lottery regional office and file a claim. The offices are located in:
Canton (216-497-5410) • Cincinnati (513•579-9603) • Cleveland (216-622-3330) • Columbus (614-466-7775) • Dayton (513-275-0872) • Lorain (216-244-3590) • Marietta (614-374-8895) • Toledo (419-245-3061) • Youngstown (216-797-2627)

Collecting Prizes

Winners have one year from the date of the drawing.

BONUS PLAY — The Kicker

This game is available in addition to Lotto 6/44. For an extra dollar, players may bet on a random generated six-digit number printed on their lotto ticket. A player who matches all six digits wins $100,000. Prizes are also awarded for matching the first two, three, four and five digits.

•Other Lottery Games•
•Pick-6 Lotto Wheeling Systems•
•Pick-3, Pick-4 Lotto Perm Systems•
•OH Subscription Agencies•
•Computer Software for OH•
•Results Line—Winning Numbers•

The Number (Pick- 3) & Pick- 4 • Instant Game
Go to pages 46-60 (Systems 14, 15, 19, 23)
Go to pages 35-45
Go to page 71
Go to pages 83-87
1-900-370-5112 ($.75 1st min, $.50 each additional min.)—go to page 89

OREGON STATE LOTTERY

✉ Oregon Lottery Headquarters
P.O.Box 12649
Salem • OR 97309

📞 *office*　(503) 378-3545

Kind of Game	## Lotto 6/44　　*Megabucks*

Bet Slip

Five boards per bet slip.

Price per Ticket

$1 for two plays per one single drawing.

How to Play

Select any 6 out of 44 numbers on one single board. Present your completed MEGABUCKS play slip to your Lotery Retailer, or insert into a Post machine. You can also ask your Lottery Retailer for "Quick Pick." The computer will then generate your numbers at random.

Drawing

Every Wednesday and Saturday at 7:28 p.m., televised statewide.

Lotto Prize Pools

All players who have matched the winning numbers, in any order, share the prize money in that category:

Prize Category	Winning Numbers Guessed Correctly	Odds (per two plays)
Jackpot	(6 out of 6)	1:3,529,526
Second Prize	(any 5 out of 6)	1:15,480
Third Prize	(any 4 out of 6)	1:335

How the $ is Divided

Oregon Lotto is a pari-mutuel game and prizes are divided equally among winners in the first three prize categories. From every dollar played, 50¢ is returned to players in the form of prizes.

Jackpot Payout

The Jackpot is paid in 20 equal annual installments when the Jackpot ($1,000,000 guaranteed) per share equals or exceeds $100,000 per year. All winnings under $100,000 are paid in a single payment.

How to Claim a Prize

Under $600 — any Lotto retailer will pay your prize;
$600 and **over** — any Lotto retailer will give you a claim form to submit to the Lottery Headquarters.

Collecting Prizes

Winners have one year from the date of the drawing.

•Other Lottery Games•
•Pick-6 Lotto Wheeling Systems•
•Daily-4 Lotto Wheeling Systems•
•Computer Software for OR•
•Results Line—Winning Numbers•

Daily-4 • Instant • LOTTO AMERICA (p
Go to pages 46-60 (Systems 14, 15, 19, 23)
Go to pages 42-45
Go to pages 83-87
1-900-370-5112 ($.75 1st min, $.50 each additional min.)—go to page 89

PENNSYLVANIA STATE LOTTERY

✉ Department of Revenue
2850 Turnpike Industrial Dr.
Middletown • PA 17057

☎ *office* (717) 986-4699
(717) 986-4700
(717) 986-4713

| Kind of Game |
| Bet Slip • Price |
| How to Play |
| Drawing |
| Lotto Prize Pools |

Lotto 6/48 *Wild Card*

Ten plays/game grids per bet slip. $1 for two plays on one ticket.

Select 6 out of 48 numbers on each single game grid. A retailer will enter your play slip into the On-Line-Terminal and print a ticket.

Every Tuesday and Friday at 7 p.m., televised statewide.

All players who have matched the numbers, in any order, share the prize money in that category:

Prize Category	Winning Numbers Guessed Correctly	Odds (per 2 plays)
First Prize	(6 out of 6)	1:6,135,756
Second Prize	(5 out of 6)+Wild Card	1:1,022,626
Third Prize	(5 out of 6)	1:24,348
Fourth Prize	(4 out of 6)+Wild Card	1:9,976.5
Fifth Prize	(4 out of 6)	1:475

| Kind of Game |
| Bet Slip • Price |
| How to Play |
| Drawing |
| Lotto Prize Pools |

Lotto 7/11/80 *Super 7*

Five plays/game grids per bet slip. $1 per one drawing.

Select any 7 out of 80 numbers on each single game grid. Any on-line retailer will process your bet slip and print you a ticket.

Wednesday at 7 p.m., televised statewide.

All players who have matched the winning numbers, in any order, share the prize money in that category:

Prize Category	Winning Numbers Guessed Correctly	Odds
Jackpot	(any 7 out of 11)	1:9,626,413
Second Prize	(any 6 out of 11)	1:99,653
Third Prize	(any 5 out of 11)	1:2,931
Third Prize ($7)	(any 4 out of 11)	1:184

General Information (applies to both games)

| Jackpot Payout |

6/48 Game—a $1,000,000 Jackpot is guaranteed and paid over a 21 year period. **7/11/80 Game**—a $2,000,000 Jackpot is guaranteed and paid over a 26 year period. Annuities—principal+interest.

| Claiming a Prize |

$2,500 or less—any retailer will pay your prize.
Over $2,500 or $2,500 or less claimed 180 days after the drawing—fill out a claim form.

| Collecting Prizes |

Winners have one year from the date of the drawing.

•Other Lottery Games•
•Pick-6 and Pick-7 Lotto Wheeling Systems•
•Pick-3, Pick-4 Lotto Perm Systems•
•PA Subscription Agencies•
•Computer Software for PA•
•Results Line—Winning Numbers•

Daily Games—Pick 3&Pick 4 • Instant Game
Go to pages 46-60 (Systems 21, 25)
Go to pages 35-45)
Go to pages 71, 74, 75
Go to pages 83-87
1-900-370-5112 ($.75 lst min, $.50 each additional min.)—go to page 89

RHODE ISLAND LOTTERY

✉ 1425 Pontiac Avenue
Cranston • RI 02920

📞 *office* (401) 463-6500

Kind of Game

Lotto 5/40   *Lot-O-Bucks*

Bet Slip

Five boards per bet slip.

Price per Ticket

$1 per one single drawing. $2 with insurance.

How to Play

Select any 5 out of 40 numbers on one single board. A Lotto retailer will enter your play slip into the On-Line Terminal, which will print a ticket.

Drawing

Every Tuesday, Thursday and Saturday at 7:29 p.m., televised statewide.

Lotto Prize Pools

All players who have matched all winning numbers, in any order, share the Jackpot prize. The remaining prize categories have fixed payouts:

Prize Category	Winning Numbers Guessed Correctly	Odds
Jackpot	(5 out of 5)	1:658,008
Second Prize ($450)	(any 4 out of 5)	1:3,760
Third Prize ($20)	(any 3 out of 5)	1:110
Fourth Prize (Free Play)	(any 2 out of 5)	1:10

How the $ is Divided

Lotto is a pari-mutuel game and the Jackpot is divided equally among winners in the first prize categories. From every dollar played, 50¢ is returned to players in the form of prizes.

Jackpot Payout

The Jackpot is paid in a lump sum when it is less than $200,000. If it is over $200,000, the prize will be paid in 11 annual installments. You can obtain claim information by calling the number above.

Advance Play

Multi-Draw lets the customer play the same numbers for 3, 6, 9, 12, or 15 consecutive drawings for no extra cost.

How to Claim a Prize

Under $450 — any Lotto retailer will pay your prize;
$450 and **over** — these prizes must be claimed at the Rhode Island Lottery's main office; a Jackpot winner should sign the ticket immediately and always claim the prize in person at any Rhode Island Lottery office.

Collecting Prizes

Winners have one year from the date of the drawing to collect.

•Other Lottery Games•
•Pick-5, 6 Lotto Wheeling Systems•
•Pick-3 and Pick-4 Lotto Wheeling Systems•
•Computer Software for RI•
•Results Line—Winning Numbers•

Pick-3 • Pick-4 • Instant • **LOTTO AMERICA** (p. 31)
Go to pages 46-60 (Systems 5, 7, 18, 22)
Go to pages 35-45
Go to pages 83-87
1-900-370-5112 ($.75 1st min, $.50 each additional min.)—go to page 89

TRI-STATE LOTTERY

✉ Maine: 219 Capitol St. • August • ME 04333
New Hampshire: Box 1217 • Concord
NH 03302-1217
Vermont: Box 420 • South Barre • VT 05670

☎ *office* (207) 289-6700

Kind of Game	## Lotto 6/40 *Megabucks*
Bet Slip	Five boards per bet slip.
Price per Ticket	$1 per single drawing.
How to Play	Select any 6 out of 40 numbers on one single board. A Lotto Retailer will enter your play slip into the On-Line Terminal, which will print a ticket.
Drawing	Every Saturday at 7:59 p.m. In Maine televised statewide, in New Hampshire televised on WMUR-TV 9, in Vermont televised on WNNE-TV and WCAX-TV.
Wheeling System Play	Play 7 numbers instead of 6—7 different combinations for $7. Play 8 numbers instead of 6—28 different combinations for $28.

Lotto Prize Pools

All players who have matched all numbers drawn, in any order, share the Jackpot:

Prize Category	Winning Numbers Guessed Correctly	Odds
Jackpot	(6 out of 6)	1:3,838,380
Second ($1,000)	(any 5 out of 6)	1:18,816
Third Prize ($40)	(any 4 out of 6)	1:456
Fourth (free play)	(any 3 out of 6)	1:32

How the $ is Divided

Lotto is a pari-mutuel game and the Jackpot is divided equally among winners. The remaining prize catories have fixed prizes. From every dollar played, 50¢ is returned to players in the form of prizes.

Jackpot Payout

The prize will be paid in 20 annual installments.

Multi-week Tickets

You can play a Season Pass Subscription.
Player from outside of the Tri-State area can play Tri-State Megabucks by calling the New Hampshire State Lottery at (603) 271-2825 and charging the subscription to their Visa or Master Card. The cost: 26 draws—$29, 52 draws—$55. Confirmations are shipped via UPS in two to three weeks.

How to Claim a Prize

Under $600 — any Lotto retailer will pay your prize;
$600 and **over** — any Lotto retailer will give you a claim form to submit to the Lottery Headquarters.

Collecting Prizes

Winners have one year from the date of the drawing to claim.

•Other Lottery Games•
•Pick-6 Lotto Wheeling Systems•
•Pick-3 and Pick-4 Lotto Wheeling Systems•
•Computer Software for Tri State•
•Results Line—Winning Numbers•

Pick-3 • Pick-4 • Instant
Go to pages 46-60
Go to pages 35-45
Go to pages 83-87
1-900-370-5112 ($.75 1st min, $.50 each additional min.)—go to page 89

WASHINGTON STATE LOTTERY

✉ 814 4th Ave.
Olympia • WA 98504-9770

☏ *office*   (206) 753-1412

THE LOTTO EDGE

| **Kind of Game** | ## Lotto 6/44 |

| **Bet Slip** | Ten boards per bet slip. |

| **Price per Ticket** | $1 per two games (boards) per one drawing. |

| **How to Play** | Select any 6 out of 44 numbers on one single board. A Lotto Retailer will enter your play slip into the On-Line Terminal, which will print a ticket. Or, let the state lottery computer pick the numbers for a "Quick Play" ticket. |

| **Drawing** | Saturday and Wednesday at 6:59 p.m., televised statewide. |

| **Lotto Prize Pools** | All players who have matched the winning numbers, in any order, share the prize money in that category: |

Prize Category	Winning Numbers Guessed Correctly	Odds
Jackpot	(6 out of 6)	1:3,529,526
Second Prize	(5 out of 6)	1:15,480
Third Prize	(4 out of 6)	1:335
Fourth Prize	(3 out of 6)	1:21

| **How the $ is Divided** | Lotto 6/44 is a pari-mutuel game and prizes are divided equally among winners in each prize category. From every dollar played, 46¢ is returned to players in the form of prizes. |

| **Jackpot Payout** | For each prize share with a cash value of $500,000 or more, the winner is paid through a 20-year annuity. For each prize share with a value of $250,001 to $499,999, the winner receives a 10-year annuity. An amount under $250,000 is paid in a single cash payment. |

| **How to Claim a Prize** | **Jackpot** winners must contact the nearest Washington Lottery Office and file a claim in person.
Any lotto retailer can pay a prize of $600 or less following the drawing. A winner of more than $600 can collect the prize at a Lottery regional office or by completing a claim form and sending it to the address above. |

| **Collecting Prizes** | Winners have 180 days from the date of the drawing to collect their prizes. |

•Other Lottery Games•
•Pick-6 Lotto Wheeling Systems•
•WA Subscription Agencies•
•Computer Software for WA•
•Results Line—Winning Numbers•
additional

Daily Game—Pick 3 • Instant Game
Go to pages 46-60 (Systems 14, 15, 19, 23)
Go to pages 35-41
Go to pages 83-87
1-900-370-5112 ($.75 1st min, $.50 each
additional min.)—go to page 89

WEST VIRGINIA LOTTERY

✉ P.O. Box 2067
Charleston • WV 25327

📞 *office* (304) 348-0500

Kind of Game	## Lotto 6/36 + EASY 8's
Bet Slip	Five boards per bet slip.
Price per Ticket	$1 per one single drawing.
How to Play	Select any 6 numbers on one single board. Any Lotto agent will enter your bet slip into the On-Line Terminal, which will print a ticket.
Drawing	Wednesday at 6:58 p.m., televised statewide.
State Wheeling System	Play 7 numbers instead of 6—7 different combinations for $7. Play 8 numbers instead of 6—28 different combinations for $28.

Lotto Prize Pools

All players who have matched all winning numbers, in any order, share the Jackpot:

Prize Category	Winning Numbers Guessed Correctly	Odds
Jackpot	(6 out of 6)	1:1,947,792
Second ($250)	(any 5 out of 6)	1:10,822
Third Prize ($20)	(any 4 out of 6)	1:299
Fourth (free play)	(any 3 out of 6)	1:24

How the $ is Divided

From every dollar played, 45¢ is returned in the form of prizes.

Jackpot Payout

The Jackpot is guaranteed at $500,000 each drawing. The prize will be paid in 20 annual installments.

How to Claim a Prize

Under $600 — any Lotto retailer will pay your prize; $600 and **over** — any Lotto retailer will give you a claim form to submit to the Lottery Commission for immediate payment.

Collecting Prizes

Winners have 180 days from the date of the drawing to collect.

EASY 8's

- It's an additional game on the bet slip for $1.
- You must play Lotto to play Easy 8's.
- Locate your Easy 8's numbers on the right hand side of the bet slip.
- Check the box "YES" under the Easy 8's number.

MATCH	WIN
The Entire Six Digit Number	$88,888
Last Five Digits in Exact Order	$8,888
Last Four Digits in Exact Order	$888
Last Three Digits in Exact Order	$88
Last Two Digits in Exact Order	$8
Last Digit	FREE PLAY

•Other Lottery Games•   Daily-3, -4 • Instant • **LOTTO AMERICA** (p. 31)
•Pick-6 Lotto Wheeling Systems•   Go to pages 46-60 (Systems 5, 9, 12, 24)
•Daily-3 and Daily-4 Lotto Wheeling Systems•   Go to pages 35-45
•WV Subscription Agencies•   Go to page 71
•Computer Software for WV•   Go to pages 83-87
•Results Line—Winning Numbers•   1-900-370-5112 ($.75 1st min, $.50 each additional min.)—go to page 89

LOTTO AMERICA

LOTTO AMERICA is a coast-to-coast multistate Lotto game conducted jointly by these states:

			Other Types of Games
Iowa State Lottery	2015 Grand Ave Des Moines • IA 50312	515-281-7900	Lotto 6/36 Instant • Pull Tabs
Kansas State Lottery	128 N. Kansas • Topeka • KS 66603	913-296-5700	Instant
Missouri St. Lottery	Box 1603 Jefferson City • MO 65102	314-751-4050	Lotto 6/44 Pick-3 • Instant
Oregon St. Lottery	Box 12649 Salem • OR 65102	503-378-3545	Lotto 6/42 Daily-4 • Instant
Rhode Island Lottery	1425 Pontiac Ave Cranston • RI 02920	401-463-6500	Lotto 5/40 Pick-4 • Instant
W. Virginia Lottery	Box 2067 Charleston •WV 25327	304-348-0500	Lotto 6/36 • Easy 8's Daily-3, 4 • Instant
D.C. St. Lottery	2101 M. Luther King Jr. Ave. Washington • DC 20020	202-433-8000	Lotto 6/39 Daily Double Lucky N. • Instant

Kind of Game

Bet Slip • Price

How to Play

Lotto 6/54

Six boards per bet slip. $1 per two plays per one single drawing.

Select any 6 out of 54 numbers on one single board. A Lotto Retailer will enter your play slip into the On-Line Terminal, which will print a ticket. Or you can request a "Quick Pick," which is a randomly generated set of numbers by the terminal.

Drawing

Wednesday and Saturday at 7:59 p.m., televised as follows:

Iowa	televised statewide	**Rhode Island**	Channel 10
Kansas	Channel 13	**West Virginia**	televised statewide
Missouri	televised statewide	**D.C.**	WHMM-TV 32
Oregon	televised statewide		

Lotto Prize Pools

All players who have matched all numbers drawn, in any order, share the prize money in that category:

Prize Category	Winning Numbers Guessed Correctly	Odds (per two plays)
Jackpot	(6 out of 6)	1:12,913,583
Second Prize	(any 5 out of 6)	1:44,839
Third Prize	(any 4 out of 6)	1:763

How the $ is Divided

Lotto is a pari-mutuel game and the prizes are divided equally among winners. From every dollar played, 45¢ is returned to players in the form of prizes.

Jackpot Payout

The Jackpot Pool is guaranteed at a minimum of $2 million. Each Jackpot share of less than $250,000 is paid in a single payment. $250,000 and more paid in 20 equal annual installments.

How to Claim a Prize

Under $600 — any Lotto retailer will pay your prize;
$600 and **over** — any Lotto retailer will give you a claim form to submit to the Lottery Headquarters.

Collecting Prizes

Winners have one year from the date of the drawing to claim their prizes.

IDAHO STATE LOTTERY

✉ P.O. Box 6537
Boise • ID 83707-6537

✆ *office* (208) 334-2600

In the general election of Nov. 8, 1988, the state of Idaho passed a referendum allowing a state lottery. A state lottery authority has since been established by the Idaho legislature. Tickets for the first game—probably an instant—should be on sale by summer.

INDIANA STATE LOTTERY

✉ not yet established

✆ *office* not yet established

In the general election of Nov. 8, 1988, the state of Indiana passed a referendum allowing a state lottery. A final decision on the type of game and start up date will be probably reached by the end of July 1989.

KENTUCKY STATE LOTTERY

✉ 6040 Dutchman's Ln.
Louisville • KY 40205-3271

✆ *office* (502) 473-1050

Tickets for Kentucky's first two lottery games went on sale April 4, 1989. Both were instant—no on-line games are now planned by the state's lottery corporation.
One of the games was an instant scratch-off ticket. The other was a special $2, two part ticket offering a traditional scratch-off game and a sweepstakes-type draw linked to the results of the Kentucky Derby.

MINNESOTA LOTTERY

✉ not yet established

✆ *office* not yet established

In the general election of Nov. 8, 1988, the state of Minnesota passed a referendum allowing a state lottery.
Minnesota hopes to start its first game in late 1989.

MONTANA STATE LOTTERY

✉ 2525 N. Montana Ave.
Helena • MT 59601

📞 *office*   (406) 444-5825

Currently the state sponsors an instant scratch-off game for $1 and a weekly televised spin show. A regional game is now being discussed with Idaho and South Dakota, and officials have expressed interest in joining LOTTO AMERICA. Montana plans to go on-line by November 1989.

SOUTH DAKOTA LOTTERY

✉ 207 E. Capitol Suite 200
Pierre • SD 57501

📞 *office*   (605) 773-5770

Currently the state sponsors an instant scratch-off game for $1 and a weekly televised spin show. A regional Lotto game is now being discussed. In other action, the legislature approved video lotteries. The maximum bet will be $2 and the maximum prize per game will be $1,000. There will be an 80 percent minimum average payback to the player.

VIRGINIA STATE LOTTERY

✉ P.O. Box 4689
Richmond • VA 23220

📞 *office*   (804) 367-9261

Virginia operates an on-line Pick-3 daily number game. Drawings are held at 7:59 p.m. (ET) Monday through Saturday. Tickets are sold 6 a.m. to 12 midnight seven days a week. The state also sponsors an instant scratch-off game for $1.

WISCONSIN STATE LOTTERY

✉ P.O. Box 8941
Madison • 53708-8941

📞 *office*   (608) 266-7777

Wisconsin State Lottery plans to go on-line in 1989. Meanwhile, an instant scratch-off game costing $1, and a pull-tab instant game costing $.50 per game, are offered.

WHEELING SYSTEMS ODDS

Lotto	8 Number System	9 Number System	10 Number System	11 Number System	12 Number System	13 Number System	14 Number System	15 Number System	16 Number System	17 Number System	18 Number System
6/30	21,206	7,096	2,828	1,285	643	346	198	119	74	48	32
6/36	69,564	23,188	9,275	4,216	2,108	1,135	649	389	243	157	105
6/38	98,596	32,865	13,146	5,976	2,988	1,609	919	552	345	223	149
6/39	116,522	38,841	15,536	7,062	3,531	1,901	1,086	652	407	264	176
6/40	137,085	45,695	18,278	8,308	4,154	2,237	1,278	767	479	310	207
6/42	187,350	62,450	24,979	11,355	5,677	3,057	1,747	1,048	655	424	283
6/44	252,109	84,036	33,615	15,279	7,640	4,114	2,351	1,410	882	570	380
6/45	290,895	96,965	38,786	17,630	8,815	4,747	2,712	1,627	1,017	658	439
6/46	334,529	111,151	44,604	20,275	10,137	5,459	3,119	1,872	1,170	757	505
6/48	438,268	146,089	58,436	26,562	13,281	7,151	4,086	2,452	1,532	992	661
6/49	499,422	166,474	66,590	30,268	15,134	8,149	4,657	2,794	1,746	1,130	753

The numbers above represents n in the odds formula 1:n. For example in the game 6/49: 499,422 means you will match all six winning numbers approximately once in 499,422 games if using an unabridged 8 number system.

LOTTO NUMBER SYSTEMS, REFERENCE TABLES & INFO

Daily Perms™, balanced Lotto Number Wheeling Systems, tracking tables and information will help you to "Play With Control, Not Guesswork." They give you the ability to analyze and track your play so that you can make the best decisions on planning your strategy.

In this chapter, I will also introduce you to my discoveries in Pick-3, Pick-4 and Pick-6 play. You can find many newly developed systems, some of which were published and tested in the national magazines, experiencing great successes.

Then you will find a table which will help you to choose which number system and lottery you would like to play, based on the number of combinations (games) and the different odds a number system requires for winning. Those players that would like to learn how to use any Pick 6 system from this book with their own selection of numbers can use the SAMPLE TABLE for Lotto games on page 46.

PICK-3 & PICK-4 GAMES

Playing six digit, giant, jackpot lotteries in many states throughout the United States can be invigorating,but many a cup of coffee has been brewed for socializing over the daily game lottery results. Although weekly or twice weekly Lotto wagering receives maximum publicity, the Pick-3 and Pick-4 games provide six excitement days a week. A 50¢ wager on the Pick-3 game can yield $250, with odds of winning being 1 in 1000. A 50¢ wager could provide upwards of $4000+ for a lucky Pick-4 player. Winnings in the Pick-4 are also sometimes pari-mutuel (i.e. based on the number of players and how much they bet.)

Overall, lottery games fall into three categories: Lotto (games ranging from Pick 5 through 10), instant games (scratch-off), and daily number games. Frustration and delight go hand in hand when most daily number game players see their evening lottery results. The profitable fun comes when you choose the correct number. This feat can be accomplished with usually lengthy data compiled by lottery commissions and independent publishers. You might go by a hunch or see something that inspires you to select specific digits. But, the disappointment grows when your guess is only one digit off from the winning number, or your order of digits is incorrect. Relax. There is a solution.

Basically, you choose a three or four digit number. If the numbers you play are drawn the day of your bet, you win! It's quite simple, but there is more than one approach to winning the collected lottery funds. Three or four digit numbers can be matched exactly as they are drawn i.e. the same sequence; in any order; with the first two digits, or the last two digits. A player may elect to combine several possible matches and game digits, or to combine several possible matches and game variations on the same lottery ticket. Naturally, the more ways you cover your numbers, the greater are your chances of winning. The following describes the type of betting for the Pick-3 game.

PICK-3

Straight — The number you select must be in the same exact order as it was drawn by the lottery. The number 456, for instance, must be played as 456 straight to receive the maximum eligible prize. Oftentimes, the payout is 500:1 with 1 in 1,000 odds of winning.

3-Way Box—This bet enables you to play any combination of three digits, two of which are alike. Let's say you play 3-Way Box **445**. If either 445 or 454 or 544 come up, you'll win. The odds are 1 in 333 and the payout is 160:1 (or $160 for a $1 bet).

6-Way Box—This bet permutes three different digits and covers all possible combinations of these digits. For example, if you pick 456;465;546;564;645 or 654, you have won. The odds are 1 in 166.67.

Front Pair or Back Pair — This bet requires matching the first or second two digits in their exact order: 456=45 Front and 56 Back. The odds of winning are 1 in 100 with a 50:1 payout. A 50¢ wager yields a $25 payout.

3-Way Combination — Three straight bets containing two of the same digits: playing 224 wins $250 for 50¢ if 224; 242 or 422 is selected. Odds are 1 in 1,000 of winning.

6-Way Combination — Six straight bets containing the same digits as those drawn in any order wins. For instance, 456 wins if 456;465;546;564;645 or 654 is drawn. A $3 minimum wager per ticket has a payout of $250 for each 50¢ bet at 500:1. Odds are 1:1,000 of winning.

Straight/Box 3-Way — A number with two of the same digits wins in a 3-way combination and/or straight if the number is drawn exactly the same as played. A $330 payout occurs for a Straight/Box win with an $80 payout for the Box win on a $1 bet. Odds are 1 in 333.33.

Straight/Box 6-Way or Straight with Back-Up — This game is played as a Straight and a 6-way Box bet. This variation of Pick-3 pays $290 while the Box pays $40 on a $1 bet.

HOW TO WIN IN THE PICK-3 GAME

Many state lotteries have set the Pick-3 systems (BOX, COMBO, etc.) in their terminals, allowing players to cover more draw possibilities. On the other hand, these systems are set for a limited number of digits, since they allow permutation of only three digits at a time. Because many of you wish to select a larger number of digits, I have developed several Pick-3 systems for individual players with a low budget, as well as several larger systems for family pools or Lotto clubs, which will help you play from four up to eight digits. The Pick-3 game is an immediate cash maker with the best lottery odds, and if you play smartly, you can make your play profitable.

Since there could be differences in the definition of the Pick-3 systems set by different state lotteries, I use the Illinois Pick-3 as a model game with most of the systems introduced in this book.

The digits used in this book were selected by the author and can be substituted by your own selection of digits. Let me show you how to provide the substitution using the first system "**PERMS 1**" as an example:

SAMPLE "PERMS"

PERMS 1   THE 5 DIGIT PICK-3 PERM

My model system looks like this:

Key Digit	Basic Digits	Type of System
A	a; b; c; d	1 Key Digit **with** the repetition of a Key Digit

STRAIGHT	AAA				
3-WAY BOX	AAa	AAb	AAc	AAd	
6-WAY BOX	Aab	Aac	Aad	Abc	Abd	Acd

To make the substitution is as easy as 1, 2, 3.

Let's say I want to play in Illinois, where the payouts are as follows:
STRAIGHT — **$250**/on 50¢ play
3-WAY BOX — **$80**/on 50¢ play
6-WAY BOX — **$40**/on 50¢ play

0 is my Key Digit; **1, 2, 4**, and **7** are my Basic Digits. To make the substitution is really simple: A = **0**
         a = **1**   b = **2**   c = **4**   d = **7**

Key Digit	Basic Digits	Type of System
0	1; 2; 4; 7	1 Key Digit **with** the repetition of a Key Digit

STRAIGHT	000				
3-WAY BOX	001	002	004	007	
6-WAY BOX	012	014	017	024	027	047

The system's cost: *$5.50 (on 50¢ play)*

Say, the winning number is **204**. In this case I will win **$40** (6-Way Box 024);
If the winning number is **200**, I will win **$80** (3-WAY BOX 002);
If the winning number is **000**, I will win **$250** (STRAIGHT 000); etc.

The system covers 49 (!) draw possibilities.

The following chart will show which draw possibilities are covered by different types of bets (by a Straight bet, 3-Way Box bets and 6-Way Box bets):

STRAIGHT covers: 000

3-WAY BOX covers: 001, 010, 100, 002, 020, 200, 004, 040, 400, 007, 070, 700

6-WAY BOX covers: 012, 021, 102, 201, 120, 210, 014, 041, 104, 401, 140, 410, 017, 710, 107, 701, 170, 710, 024, 042, 204, 402, 240, 420, 027, 072, 207, 702, 270, 720, 047, 740, 407, 704, 470 and 740.

If I played all the numbers above as "STRAIGHT" bets, the payout would be $250 on a 50¢ play, but I would have to spend $24.50, which certainly might be too expensive for any single player. By using **PERMS 1**, I am saving $19 per drawing. On the other hand, the winnings are lower than in the first case, as shown above.

Can I use PERMS 1 in any state?

Most U.S. lotteries have set Straight, 3-Way Box and 6-Way Box in their terminals, which enables you to use the system almost anywhere across the country. Just pick your own digits, make the substitutions and play.

But let's say that you play in a state which does not have a 3-Way Box bet, can you use PERMS 1? Of course you can!

Suppose you want to play **8** as your Key Digit and then **3, 5, 7,** and **9** as your Basic Digits.

Key Digit	Basic Digits	Type of System
8	3; 5; 7; 9	1 Key Digit **with** the repetition of a Key Digit

STRAIGHT   888

3-WAY BOX is played as *STRAIGHT* bets:

       883, 838, 388, 885, 858, 588, 887, 878, 788, 889, 898, 988

6-WAY BOX   835   837   839   857   859   879

The cost: *$19 (on $1 play)*

My favorite selection of PICK-3 PERMS

PERMS 2 — THE 5 DIGIT PICK-3 PERM

3 x 6-WAY BOX

Key Pair Digits	Basic Digits	Type of System
4, 5	1; 2; 3	Key Pair Digits **without** the repetition of digits

451   452   453

PERMS 3 — THE 6 DIGIT PICK-3 PERM

24 Straights or the four 6-WAY BOX bets

Key Pair Digits	Basic Digits	Type of System
6; 9	0; 3; 5; 7	Key Pair Digits **without** the repetition of digits

690   960   609   906   069   096   693   963   639   936   369   396
695   965   659   956   569   596   697   967   679   976   769   796

*PERMS 3 can also be played as a **6-WAY BOX** or **6-WAY COMBO** of the following digits:*
690   693   695   697

PERMS 4 — THE 7 DIGIT PICK-3 PERM

10 Straights

Key Digits	Basic Digits	Type of System
78; 87	0; 1; 2; 3; 4	2 Reverse Front Key Digits **without** the repetition of digits

780   781   782   783   784
870   871   872   873   874

PERMS 5 — THE 7 DIGIT PICK-3 PERM

10 Straights

Key Digits	Basic Digits	Type of System
12; 21	5; 6; 7; 8; 9	2 Reverse Back Key Digits **without** the repetition of digits

512   612   712   812   912
521   621   721   821   921

PERMS 6 — THE 5 DIGIT PICK-3 PERM

6-WAY BOX bets

Key Digit	Basic Digits	Type of System
6	4; 5; 7; 8	1 Key Digit **without** the repetition of digits

645   647   648   657   658   678

PERMS 7 — THE 6 DIGIT PICK-3 PERM

24 Straights

Key Digits	Basic Digits	Type of System
46; 64; 44; 66	0; 5; 8; 9	Reverse Front Key Digits **with** the repetition of the Key Digits

460	465	468	469	640	645	648	649
440	445	448	449	660	665	668	669
444	446	464	466	644	646	664	666

PERMS 8 — THE 6 DIGIT PICK-3 PERM

24 Straights

Key Digits	Basic Digits	Type of System
23; 32; 22; 33	0; 5; 7; 9	Reverse Back Key Digits **with** the repetition of the Key Digits

023	523	723	923	032	532	732	932
022	522	722	922	033	533	733	933
222	322	223	323	232	332	233	333

PERMS 9 — THE 5 DIGIT PICK-3 PERM

You can play either **$6.50**   *(on **50¢** per STRAIGHT play, on **50¢** per 3-WAY BOX, and on **50¢** per 6-WAY BOX)*

or **$22**   *(on **50¢** per STRAIGHT play, on **$1.50** per 3-WAY COMBO , and on **$3** per 6-WAY COMBO)*

Key Digits	Basic Digits	Type of System
5; 7	1; 8; 9	2 Key Digits **with** the repetition of the Key Digits

STRAIGHT: 555   777
6-WAY BOX (COMBO)   571   578   579
3-WAY BOX (COMBO)   551   558   559   771   778   779   557   775

PERMS 10   **THE 8 DIGIT PICK-3 PERM**

You can play either *$7.50*   (on *50¢* per the *3-WAY BOX* play)
or *$22.50*   (on *$1.50* per *3-WAY COMBO* play)

Key Digits	Basic Digits	Type of System
33; 66; 99	0; 4; 5; 7; 8	3 x Same Key Digits + 5 Basic Digits

3-WAY BOX (COMBO):

330	334	335	337	338
660	664	665	667	668
990	994	995	997	998

Playing double and triple numbers

By playing double and triple numbers, you can reduce the field from which you choose to 280 numbers. Although it is self-evident that any number has the same chance to be drawn, even repeated several times in a row, many players eliminate the most frequently drawn digits and pick the digits that have not appeared for several drawings. Then they play a full permutation of these digits. For example, the system for any two digits **a,b** looks like this:

My Model Number	Selected Digits	Substitution	Numbers	Played
aab	2	a = 2	**228**	[aab]
aba	8	b = 8	**282**	[aba]
baa			**822**	[baa]
bba			**882**	[bba]
bab			**828**	[bab]
abb			**288**	[abb]
aaa			**222**	[aaa]
bbb			**888**	[bbb]

Do you need a larger selection of the Pick-3 and Pick-4 Number Systems ?

If you need a larger selection of *PERMS™* with detailed Prize Guarantees, you can find **10** of these systems in the *"Daily Perm Pack—An Immediate Cash Maker"* by Robert Serotic (First Edition, 1989), published by L.S.I. Publishing, Inc., 1259 El Camino Real, Suite 217, Menlo Park, CA 94025.

This set of the most powerful systems will bring you many proven *PERMS™* that will satisfy players with a low weekly Lotto budget! It also introduces several larger Pick-3 systems suitable for Lotto Clubs and Family Pools.

All newly developed systems and methods for Pick-3 and Pick-4 play are published in my monthly newsletter *"LOTTO ADVISOR U.S.A."* You can order a free copy of this helpful publication by calling Customer Service 408/980-1999.

PICK-4

Straight — Choosing a four digit number that is drawn exactly as you play it, in the same order, wins. It must be an exact match. The payout, generally, is $5000 per $1 bet. Pari-mutuel drawings vary the prize(s), and the winnings can sometimes be less or sometimes more. Odds are 1 in 10,000.

4-Way Box — Three of the same digits in a four digit number, played in any order wins. Playing 1112 wins if 1112; 1121; 1211; or 2111 is drawn. Odds are 1 in 2,500 of winning, with a $1,250 payout per $1 bet.

6-Way Box — Playing a four digit number containing the same two digits drawn in any order wins! If you play 2233 and 2233; 2323; 2332; 3223; 3232; or 3322 is drawn, you win. Odds are 1 in 667 with an 800:1 payout.

12-Way Box — Covers all draw possibilities of a four digit number with two of the same digits. Let's say you play 1123 — if 1123; 1132; 1213; 1231; 1321; 1312; 2311; 2113; 2131; 3211; 3112; or 3121 is drawn, you win! Odds are 1 in 833 with a $400:$1 payout.

24-Way Box — Permutes four different digits in any order to cover all draw possibilities. Odds are 1 in 417 with a $200:$1 payout.

My favorite selection of PICK-4 PERMS

P-4 PERMS 1

Key Pair Digits	Basic Digits	Type of System
—	4; 5; 1; 2	4 Basic Digits **without** the repetition of digits

This system can be played two different ways:

Play either **24 Straights**

The system cost is $12 on a 50¢ play; the payout is $2,500 on a 50¢ play if 4; 5; 1; 2 are drawn in any order:

4512	4521	4152	4251	4125	4215	5412	5421	5142	5241	5124	5214
1452	2451	1425	2415	1245	2145	1542	2541	1524	2514	1254	2154

or play **1x 24-WAY BOX**

Play **one** ticket: 4512

The cost is 50¢; the payout is $100 on 50¢ ticket when 4; 5; 1; 2 are drawn in any order.

P-4 PERMS 2

Key Pair Digits	Basic Digits	Type of System
37; 73	2; 4; 6	2 Key Pair Digits **without** the repetition of digits

You can play either **72 Straights**

The system cost is $36 on a 50¢ play. The payout is $2,500 on 50¢ if you guess correctly any of the following numbers:

3724	3742	3274	3472	3247	3427		7324	7342	7234	7432	7243	7423
2374	4372	2347	4327	2437	4237		2734	4732	2743	4723	2473	4273
3726	3762	3276	3672	3267	3627		7326	7362	7236	7632	7263	7623
2376	6372	2367	6327	2637	6237		2736	6732	2763	6723	2673	6273
3746	3764	3476	3674	3467	3647		7346	7364	7436	7634	7463	7643
4376	6374	4367	6347	4637	6437		4736	6734	4763	6743	4673	6473

or play **3 x 24-WAY BOX**

Play **three** tickets: 3724   3726   3746

The cost is only $1.50 on a 50¢ play, but the payout is much lower — $100 on a 50¢ play when you guess correctly any Key Pair Digits + any 2 Basic Digits.

P-4 PERMS 3   **6x 12-WAY BOX**

The cost is $3 on a 50¢ play and the payout is $100 when you guess correctly any **1** Key Pair Same Digits + any 2 Basic Digits.

Key Pairs Same Digits	Basic Digits	Type of System
00; 11	3; 6; 7	2 Key Pair Same Digits **without** the repetition of digits

6 x *12-WAY BOX* tickets: 0036   0037   0067   1136   1137   1167

P-4 PERMS 4   **18x 12-WAY BOX**

The cost is $9 and the payout is $200 on a 50¢ play. You will win if you guess correctly any **1** Key Pair Same Digits + any 2 different Basic Digits.

Key Pair Same Digits	Basic Digits	Type of System
11; 55; 88	1; 2; 3; 5; 8	3 Key Pair Same Digits without the repetition of digits

6 *12-WAY BOX* tickets:	1123	1125	1128	1135	1138	1158
6 *12-WAY BOX* tickets:	5512	5513	5518	5523	5528	5538
6 *12-WAY BOX* tickets:	8812	8813	8815	8823	8825	8835

P-4 PERMS 5   4x 4-WAY BOX + 6 x 12-WAY BOX

You will win either a **4-WAY BOX** if you guess correctly the Key Triple Same Digits + any Basic Digit, or **12-WAY BOX** if you guess correctly any 2 Key Pair Same Digits + any 2 Basic Digits. The cost is $5 and the payout is $600 or $200 on a 50¢ play.

Key Triple Same Digits	Basic Digits	Type of System
222	4; 5; 8; 9	Key Triple Same Digits without the repetition of digits

4x *4-WAY BOX* tickets:	2224	2225	2228	2229	
6x *12-WAY BOX* tickets:	2245	2248	2249	2258	2259	2289

P-4 PERMS 6   18x 12-WAY BOX

You will win a **12-WAY BOX** if you guess correctly any Key Pair Same Digits + any 2 Basic Digits. **Basic conditions:** 2 odd + 2 even digits must be drawn. The cost is $10 and the payout is $200 on a 50¢ play.

Key Pair Same Digits	Basic Digits	Type of System
66; 99	0; 1; 2; 3; 4; 5; 6; 7; 8; 9	2 Key Pair Same Digits without the repetition of digits

12-WAY BOX 6613 6615 6617 6619 6635 6637 6639 6657 6659 6679
6350 9902 9904 9906 9908 9924 9926 9928 9946 9948 9968

P-4 SYSTEM 7   9x 24-WAY BOX

You will win a **24-WAY BOX** if you guess correctly the Key Digit **9** + any **3** Basic Digits. **Basic condition:** 2 odd + 2 even digits **must be drawn**. The cost is $5 and the payout is $100 on a 50¢ play.

Key Digit	Basic Digits	Type of System
9	3; 4; 5; 6; 7; 8	1 Key Digit + 6 Basic Digits **without** the repetition of digits

9x **24-WAY BOX** plays: 9346 9348 9368
9546 9548 9568
9746 9748 9768

P-4 PERMS 8   15x 24-WAY BOX

You will win a **24-WAY BOX** if you guess correctly any **4** Basic Digits. The cost is $7.50 and the payout is $100 on a 50¢ play.

Key Digit	Basic Digits	Type of System
—	4; 5; 6; 7; 8; 9	6 Consecutive Basic Digits **without** the repetition of digits

15x 24-WAY BOX plays:

4567	4568	4569	4578	4579
4589	4678	4679	4689	4789
5678	5679	5689	5789	6789

P-4 PERMS 9   10x 24-WAY BOX + 10x 12-WAY BOX + 5x 4-WAY BOX + 1 STRAIGHT

The system's cost is $12.50 on a 50¢ play, and the payout varies with the number guessed.

Key Digit	Basic Digits	Type of System
7	0; 2; 4; 6; 8	1 Key Digit + 5 Basic Digits **with** the repetition of the Key digit

10x 24-WAY BOX plays:

7024	7026	7028	7046	7048	7068
7246	7248	7268	7468		

10x 12-WAY BOX plays:

7702	7704	7706	7708	7724	7726
7728	7746	7748	7768		

10x 4-WAY BOX plays:

7770	7772	7774	7776	7778

1x STRAIGHT .   7777

From computer generated astrological data and cyclical number analysis to Quick Picks and just plain intuition, there are many ways of selecting your Pick-3 & Pick-4 lottery numbers. Whether it is the phase of the moon or a formal statistical analysis of probabilities based on lottery number histories, millions of dollars are won by Pick-3 and Pick-4 players annually. So, Good Luck Winners!

Never bet more than 5% of your net weekly income!

My favorite selection of PICK-6 SYSTEMS

SAMPLE TABLE FOR PICK 6 LOTTO

The following Sample Table will help you to easily substitute your numbers into any system, construct a system with your numbers, and then you can fill in your games on the Bet Slips.

There are many systems in this book that can be used for any kind of Lotto game anywhere around the world. Every system has a well balanced selection of numbers and can be used as is.

But what do you do if you want a system that was selected for a different state and you want to play it in your state? Or you want to play your own numbers instead of the pre-selected ones. Can you do it? Of course you can , and it is simple in either case. Let me show you the procedure, using for example, the following System 4 selected for the Delaware 6/36 game.

System 4 THE 10 NUMBER COMBINATION

Second Prize (5 out of 6) is guaranteed if all 6 winning numbers are among the 10 selected numbers. The odds of having all 6 winning numbers among the 10 selected numbers are 1:6,404.

P6/6 = 7.1%   *15 games*

LP+ Selection	2	5	8	12	15	18	22	25	28	32
YOUR #'s										

1. 2 5 8 12 15 18	*6.* 2 8 12 25 28 32	*11.* 5 8 15 22 28 32
2. 2 5 8 22 25 28	*7.* 2 15 18 22 25 28	*12.* 5 12 15 22 25 28
3. 2 5 12 18 28 32	*8.* 2 15 18 25 28 32	*13.* 5 12 15 22 25 32
4. 2 5 18 22 25 32	*9.* 5 8 12 15 22 25	*14.* 8 12 18 22 25 28
5. 2 8 12 15 22 32	*10.* 5 8 15 18 25 32	*15.* 8 12 18 22 28 32

Suppose you want to use this system for the Michigan 6/44 game. Can you do it? Of course, you can! Let's say your selection is:

3   8   14   22   23   25   26   33   39   44

Enter the numbers you wish to play in the row **YOUR #'s**:

LP+ Selection	2	5	8	12	15	18	22	25	28	32
YOUR #'s	*3*	*8*	*14*	*22*	*23*	*25*	*26*	*33*	*39*	*44*

and make the substitution of your numbers. When the substitutions are made, **YOUR SYSTEM** should look like this:

1. 3 8 14 22 23 25	*6.* 3 14 22 33 39 44	*11.* 8 14 23 26 39 44
2. 3 8 14 26 33 39	*7.* 3 23 25 26 33 39	*12.* 8 22 23 26 33 39
3. 3 8 22 25 39 44	*8.* 3 23 25 33 39 44	*13.* 8 22 23 26 33 44
4. 3 8 25 26 33 44	*9.* 8 14 22 23 26 33	*14.* 14 22 25 26 33 39
5. 3 14 22 23 26 44	*10.* 8 14 23 25 33 44	*15.* 14 22 25 26 39 44

AZ 6/39 (until June 30, 1989)—*A wheeling system that reduces the odds to* **1:407**

System 1 THE 16 NUMBER COMBINATION

Fourth Prize (4 out of 6) is guaranteed if 6 winning numbers are among the 16 selected numbers. The odds of having all 6 winning numbers among the 16 selected numbers are 1:407.

P6/6 = 0.41%   *33 games*

You can play either the following numbers or replace them with your favorite numbers:

LP+ Selection	2	7	10	14	16	19	21	25
YOUR #'s								

LP+ Selection	28	29	31	34	35	37	38	39
YOUR #'s								

1. 2 7 10 14 35 37	*12.* 2 14 19 21 10 31	*23.* 16 19 21 25 35 39
2. 2 7 10 14 35 38	*13.* 7 10 16 25 10 31	*24.* 16 19 21 25 37 38
3. 2 7 10 14 35 39	*14.* 7 10 19 21 28 34	*25.* 16 19 21 25 37 39
4. 2 7 10 14 37 38	*15.* 7 14 16 21 10 34	*26.* 16 19 21 25 38 39
5. 2 7 10 14 37 39	*16.* 7 14 19 25 28 31	*27.* 28 10 31 34 35 37
6. 2 7 10 14 38 39	*17.* 7 16 21 34 37 39	*28.* 28 10 31 34 35 38
7. 2 7 16 19 28 10	*18.* 10 14 16 19 31 34	*29.* 28 10 31 34 35 39
8. 2 7 21 25 31 34	*19.* 10 14 21 25 28 10	*30.* 28 10 31 37 38 39
9. 2 10 16 21 28 31	*20.* 14 16 28 10 34 38	*31.* 28 34 35 37 38 39
10. 2 10 19 25 10 34	*21.* 16 19 21 25 35 37	*32.* 10 34 35 37 38 39
11. 2 14 16 25 28 34	*22.* 16 19 21 25 35 38	*33.* 31 34 35 37 38 39

CA, FL 6/49—*A wheeling system that reduces the odds to* **1:753**

System 2 THE 18 NUMBER COMBINATION

Fifth Prize (3 out of 6) is guaranteed if 5 winning numbers are among the 18 selected numbers. The odds of having all 6 winning numbers among the 18 selected numbers are 1:753.

P6/6 = 0.06%   *12 games*

You can play either the following numbers or replace them with your favorite numbers:

LP+ Selection	4	13	16	18	21	24	26	30	32
YOUR #'s									

LP+ Selection	37	38	39	41	43	44	46	48	49
YOUR #'s									

1. 4 13 16 18 21 24	*5.* 16 18 26 30 41 43	*9.* 21 24 32 37 38 39
2. 4 13 26 30 32 37	*6.* 16 18 32 37 44 46	*10.* 21 24 41 43 44 46
3. 4 13 38 39 41 43	*7.* 16 18 38 39 48 49	*11.* 26 30 38 39 44 46
4. 4 13 44 46 48 49	*8.* 21 24 26 30 48 49	*12.* 32 37 41 43 48 49

CT, NY, TRI STATE 6/40—*A wheeling system that reduces the odds to 1:99*

System 3   THE 20 NUMBER COMBINATION

*Third Prize (4 out of 6) is guaranteed if **both** Key Numbers + any 3 winning numbers are among the 20 selected numbers. The odds of having all 6 winning numbers among the 20 selected numbers are 1:99.*

P6/6 = 0.5%   15 games

You can play either the following numbers or replace them with your favorite numbers:

	KEY #'s						
LP+ Selection	15	40	3	4	6	11	13
YOUR #'s							

LP+ Selection	16	19	21	24	25	26	29
YOUR #'s							

LP+ Selection	30	32	35	36	38	39
YOUR #'s						

1. 15 40 3 6 19 21
2. 15 40 3 13 29 30
3. 15 40 3 32 36 39
4. 15 40 4 11 16 24
5. 15 40 4 11 25 38
6. 15 40 4 25 26 35
7. 15 40 6 13 19 32
8. 15 40 6 19 29 36
9. 15 40 6 19 30 39
10. 15 40 11 16 26 35
11. 15 40 13 21 36 39
12. 15 40 16 24 25 38
13. 15 40 21 29 30 32
14. 15 40 24 26 35 38
15. 15 40 29 30 36 39

D.C., DE, IO, MA, WV 6/36—*A wheeling system that reduces the odds to 1:9,275*

System 4   THE 10 NUMBER COMBINATION

Second Prize (5 out of 6) is guaranteed if all 6 winning numbers are among the 10 selected numbers. The odds of having all 6 winning numbers among the 10 selected numbers are 1:6,404.

P6/6 = 7.1%   15 games

You can play either the following numbers or replace them with your favorite numbers:

LP+ Selection	2	5	8	12	15	18	22	25	28	32
YOUR #'s										

1. 2 5 8 12 15 18
2. 2 5 8 22 25 28
3. 2 5 12 18 28 32
4. 2 5 18 22 25 32
5. 2 8 12 15 22 32
6. 2 8 12 25 28 32
7. 2 15 18 22 25 28
8. 2 15 18 25 28 32
9. 5 8 12 15 22 25
10. 5 8 15 18 25 32
11. 5 8 15 22 28 32
12. 5 12 15 22 25 28
13. 5 12 15 22 25 32
14. 8 12 18 22 25 28
15. 8 12 18 22 28 32

D.C., DE, IO, MA, WV 6/36—*A wheeling system that reduces the odds to 1:1,135*

System 5   THE 13 NUMBER COMBINATION

Third Prize (4 out of 6) is guaranteed if all 6 winning numbers are among the 13 selected numbers. The odds of having all 6 winning numbers among the 13 selected numbers are 1:1,135.

P6/6 = 0.7%   *12 games*

You can play either the following numbers or replace them with your favorite numbers:

LP+ Selection	2	6	13	17	20	23	26
YOUR #'s							

LP+ Selection	28	29	31	33	35	36
YOUR #'s						

1. 2 6 13 20 23 26	*5.* 2 28 31 33 35 36	*9.* 6 13 17 33 35 36
2. 2 6 17 20 23 26	*6.* 2 29 31 33 35 36	*10.* 20 23 26 28 29 31
3. 2 13 17 20 23 26	*7.* 6 13 17 20 23 26	*11.* 20 23 26 33 35 36
4. 2 28 29 33 35 36	*8.* 6 13 17 28 29 31	*12.* 26 28 29 31 33 35

FL, CA 6/49—*A wheeling system that reduces the odds to 1:753*

System 6   THE 18 NUMBER COMBINATION

Fifth Prize (3 out of 6) is guaranteed if 5 winning numbers are among the 18 selected numbers. The odds of having all 6 winning numbers among the 18 selected numbers are 1:753.

P6/6 = 0.06%   *12 games*

You can play either the following numbers or replace them with your favorite numbers:

LP+ Selection	2	5	8	15	17	18	20	21	22
YOUR #'s									

LP+ Selection	25	32	33	35	38	40	47	48	49
YOUR #'s									

1. 2 5 8 15 17 18	*5.* 8 15 20 21 35 38	*9.* 17 18 22 25 32 33
2. 2 5 20 21 22 25	*6.* 8 15 22 25 40 47	*10.* 17 18 35 38 40 47
3. 2 5 32 33 35 38	*7.* 8 15 32 33 48 49	*11.* 20 21 32 33 40 47
4. 2 5 40 47 48 49	*8.* 17 18 20 21 48 49	*12.* 22 25 35 38 48 49

IL, NY, LOTTO AMERICA 6/54—*A system that reduces the odds to 1:192*

System 7   THE 24 NUMBER COMBINATION

Third Prize (4 out of 6) is guaranteed if all both Key Numbers + any 3 winning numbers are among the 24 selected numbers. The odds of having all 6 winning numbers among the 24 selected numbers are 1:192.

P6/6 = 0.2%   21 games

You can play either the following numbers or replace them with your favorite numbers:

	KEY #'s						
LP+ Selection	27	54	2	4	8	15	18	21
YOUR #'s							

LP+ Selection	24	25	29	30	33	35	36	39
YOUR #'s							

LP+ Selection	40	42	45	48	49	50	51	53
YOUR #'s							

1. 27 54 2 8 15 35	*8.* 27 54 4 42 49 51	*15.* 27 54 18 24 25 49
2. 27 54 2 21 29 33	*9.* 27 54 8 21 39 40	*16.* 27 54 18 24 42 51
3. 27 54 2 39 45 50	*10.* 27 54 8 29 45 48	*17.* 27 54 21 35 45 53
4. 27 54 2 40 48 53	*11.* 27 54 8 33 50 53	*18.* 27 54 24 25 36 42
5. 27 54 4 18 24 30	*12.* 27 54 15 21 48 50	*19.* 27 54 29 35 40 50
6. 27 54 4 18 36 51	*13.* 27 54 15 29 39 53	*20.* 27 54 30 36 42 49
7. 27 54 4 25 30 51	*14.* 27 54 15 33 40 45	*21.* 27 54 33 35 39 48

IL 5/35—*A Pick 5 wheeling system that reduces the odds to 1:410*
FL 5/39—*A Pick 5 wheeling system that reduces the odds to 1:727*
RI 5/40—*A Pick 5 wheeling system that reduces the odds to 1:830*

System 8   THE 12 NUMBER COMBINATION

Third Prize (3 out of 5) is guaranteed if any 4 winning numbers are among the 12 selected numbers. The odds of having all 5 winning numbers among the 12 selected numbers are 1:410.

P5/5 = 1.5%   12 games

You can play either the following numbers or replace them with your favorite numbers:

LP+ Selection	1	6	7	14	17	22
YOUR #'s						

LP+ Selection	25	27	28	32	34	35
YOUR #'s						

1. 1 6 7 25 28	*5.* 1 25 32 34 35	*9.* 7 17 28 32 35
2. 1 6 14 22 35	*6.* 6 7 14 27 32	*10.* 7 22 25 27 35
3. 1 7 14 17 34	*7.* 6 17 22 25 34	*11.* 14 17 25 27 28
4. 1 17 22 27 32	*8.* 6 27 28 34 35	*12.* 14 22 28 32 34

D.C., DE, IO, MA, WV 6/36—*A wheeling system that reduces the odds to 1:389*

System 9   THE 15 NUMBER COMBINATION

Fourth Prize (4 out of 6) is guaranteed if both Key Numbers + any 4 winning numbers are among the 15 selected numbers. The odds of having all 6 winning numbers among the 15 selected numbers are 1:389.

P6/6 = 1.8%   *13 games*

You can play either the following numbers or replace them with your favorite numbers:

	KEY #'s							
LP+ Selection	**5**	**34**	**4**	**7**	**10**	**16**	**19**	**22**
YOUR #'s								

LP+ Selection	**23**	**26**	**28**	**29**	**31**	**35**	**36**
YOUR #'s							

1. 5 34 4 7 10 28
2. 5 34 4 16 19 22
3. 5 34 4 23 31 35
4. 5 34 4 26 29 36
5. 5 34 7 16 23 29

6. 5 34 7 19 26 35
7. 5 34 7 22 31 36
8. 5 34 10 16 35 36
9. 5 34 10 19 29 31

10. 5 34 10 22 23 26
11. 5 34 16 26 28 31
12. 5 34 19 23 28 36
13. 5 34 22 28 29 35

CT, NY, TRI STATE 6/40—*A wheeling system that reduces the odds to 1:4,154*

System 10   THE 12 NUMBER COMBINATION

Fourth Prize (4 out of 6) is guaranteed if one Key Number + any 4 winning numbers are among the 12 selected numbers. The odds of having all 6 winning numbers among the 12 selected numbers are 1:4,154.

P6/6 = 1.95%   *9 games*

You can play either the following numbers or replace them with your favorite numbers:

	KEY #					
LP+ Selection	**40**	**3**	**8**	**13**	**18**	**22**
YOUR #'s						

LP+ Selection	**25**	**29**	**32**	**35**	**37**	**38**
YOUR #'s						

1. 40 3 8 13 18 32
2. 40 3 13 18 29 32
3. 40 3 13 18 32 38

4. 40 3 22 25 35 37
5. 40 8 22 29 37 38
6. 40 8 25 29 35 38

7. 40 13 22 25 35 37
8. 40 18 22 25 35 37
9. 40 22 25 32 35 37

MD, MI, MO, OH, OR, WA 6/40
—A wheeling system that reduces the odds to 1:479

System 11 THE 16 NUMBER COMBINATION

Third Prize (4 out of 6) is guaranteed if one Key Number + 1 winning number from each Group are among the six winning numbers. The odds of having all 6 winning numbers among the 16 selected numbers are 1:479.

P6/6 = 3.7% 9 games

You can play either the following numbers or replace them with your favorite numbers:

Key #	GROUP 1			GROUP 2			GROUP 3		
39	13	23	33	14	24	34	15	25	35

GROUP 4			GROUP 5		
16	26	36	18	28	38

1. 39 13 14 15 16 18	*4.* 39 23 14 25 36 38	*7.* 39 33 14 35 26 28
2. 39 13 24 25 26 38	*5.* 39 23 24 35 16 28	*8.* 39 33 24 15 36 18
3. 39 13 34 35 36 28	*6.* 39 23 34 15 26 18	*9.* 39 33 34 25 16 38

D.C., DE, IO, MA, WV 6/36
—A wheeling system that reduces the odds to 1:2,108

System 12 THE 12 NUMBER COMBINATION

Second Prize (5 out of 6) is guaranteed if 1 number from each Group is among the 6 winning numbers. The odds of having all 6 winning numbers among the 12 selected numbers are 1:2,108.

P6/6 = 18.7% 12 games

You can play either the following numbers or replace them with your favorite numbers:

	Group 1		Group 2		Group 3	
LP+ Selection	1	2	14	15	20	21
YOUR #'s						

	Group 4		Group 5		Group 6	
LP+ Selection	27	28	31	32	35	36
YOUR #'s						

1. 1 14 20 27 31 35	*5.* 1 15 20 27 32 36	*9.* 1 15 21 27 31 36
2. 1 14 21 28 32 36	*6.* 1 15 20 28 31 36	*10.* 1 15 21 28 32 35
3. 2 15 20 27 31 35	*7.* 2 14 21 27 32 35	*11.* 2 14 20 27 31 36
4. 2 15 21 28 32 36	*8.* 2 14 21 28 31 35	*12.* 2 14 20 28 32 35

You can use System 12 at any World Race Track for the Horse Racing Pick-Six game*.

When **Horse Racing Pick Six** is played:
Each Group represents one race. Pick 2 horses in each race. You will play 12 horses total. Pick Five (5 out of 6) is guaranteed if six daily winners are among the 12 horses you play.

	Race 1		Race 2		Race 3	
LP+ Selection	7	13	2	4	2	10
YOUR #'s						

	Race 4		Race 5		Race 6	
LP+ Selection	3	9	1	2	5	8
YOUR #'s						

1. 7 2 2 3 1 5	*5.* 7 4 2 3 2 8	*9.* 7 4 10 3 1 8
2. 7 2 10 9 2 8	*6.* 7 4 2 9 1 8	*10.* 7 4 10 9 2 5
3. 13 4 2 3 1 5	*7.* 13 2 10 3 2 5	*11.* 13 2 2 3 1 8
4. 13 4 10 9 2 8	*8.* 13 2 10 9 1 5	*12.* 13 2 2 9 2 5

* You can find more interesting Horse Racing Pick-Six, Pick-Nine and Triple Systems in the book *"Horseracing — Pick Six and Pick Nine Systems"* by James Love and Robert Serotic, to be published by L.S.I. Publishing, 1259 El Camino Real, Suite 217, Menlo Park, CA 94025.

MA, NJ 6/46—*A wheeling system that reduces the odds to 1:1,872*

System 13   ## THE 15 NUMBER COMBINATION

Second Prize (5 out of 6) is guaranteed if 3 Key Numbers + any 3 numbers from the 12 selected numbers are among the 6 winning numbers. The odds of having all 6 winning numbers among the 15 selected numbers are 1:1,872.

                              P6/6 = 5%   *11 games*

You can play either the following numbers or replace them with your favorite numbers:

	Key Numbers							
LP+ Selection	14	24	46	1	7	16	21	26
YOUR #'s								

LP+ Selection	31	35	36	40	41	44	45
YOUR #'s							

1. 14 24 46 1 16 26	*5.* 14 24 46 7 35 45	*9.* 14 24 46 26 31 40
2. 14 24 46 1 31 44	*6.* 14 24 46 16 31 36	*10.* 14 24 46 26 36 44
3. 14 24 46 1 36 40	*7.* 14 24 46 16 40 44	*11.* 14 24 46 35 41 45
4. 14 24 46 7 21 41	*8.* 14 24 46 21 35 45	

MD, MI, MO, OH, OR, WA 6/44—*A system that reduces the odds to 1:7,640*

System 14   THE 12 NUMBER COMBINATION

Third Prize (4 out of 6) is guaranteed if **any** *5 numbers from the 12 selected numbers is among the 6 winning numbers. The odds of having all 6 winning numbers among the 12 selected numbers are 1:7,640.*   *P6/6 = 1.3%*   *18 games*

You can play either the following numbers or replace them with your favorite numbers:

LP+ Selection	3	8	14	17	22	27
YOUR #'s						

LP+ Selection	30	31	34	35	41	44
YOUR #'s						

1. 3   8 17 22 30 35
2. 3   8 17 30 31 35
3. 3   8 17 30 35 41
4. 3 14 17 27 34 44
5. 3 14 27 30 34 44
6. 3 14 27 34 35 44

7. 3 17 22 30 31 35
8. 3 17 22 30 35 41
9. 3 17 30 31 35 41
10. 8 14 22 27 31 41
11. 8 14 22 31 34 41
12. 8 14 22 31 41 44

13. 8 22 27 31 34 41
14. 8 22 27 31 41 44
15. 8 22 31 34 41 44
16. 14 17 27 30 34 44
17. 14 17 27 34 35 44
18. 14 27 30 34 35 44

MD, MI, MO, OH, OR, WA 6/44—*A wheeling system that reduces the odds to 1:19*

System 15   THE 28 NUMBER COMBINATION

Third Prize (4 out of 6) is guaranteed if **both** *Key Numbers + any 4 numbers from the 28 selected numbers are among the 6 winning numbers. The odds of having all 6 winning numbers among the 15 selected numbers are 1:19.*   *P6/6 = 0.14%*   *21 games*   **$10.50**

You can play either the following numbers or replace them with your favorite numbers:

LP+ Selection	Key Numbers							
	16	41	1	2	4	7	8	9	10
YOUR #'s									

LP+ Selection	13	15	17	18	20	22	24	27	28	30
YOUR #'s										

LP+ Selection	31	33	36	37	38	40	42	43	44
YOUR #'s									

1. 16 41   1   7 17 18
2. 16 41   1 11 27 37
3. 16 41   1 36 40 44
4. 16 41   2 10 15 24
5. 16 41   2 10 22 33
6. 16 41   2 22 31 42
7. 16 41   4   8 13 28

8. 16 41   4   8 20 38
9. 16 41   4 20 30 43
10. 16 41   7 11 18 36
11. 16 41   7 18 27 40
12. 16 41   7 18 37 44
13. 16 41   8 13 30 43
14. 16 41 10 15 31 42

15. 16 41 11 17 40 44
16. 16 41 13 20 28 38
17. 16 41 15 22 24 33
18. 16 41 17 27 36 37
19. 16 41 24 31 33 42
20. 16 41 27 37 40 44
21. 16 41 28 30 38 43

CO 6/42—*A wheeling system that reduces the odds to **1:1,048***

System 16   THE 15 NUMBER COMBINATION

*Third Prize (4 out of 6) is guaranteed if **one** Key Number + any 5 numbers from the 15 selected numbers are among the 6 winning numbers.*
The odds of having all 6 winning numbers among the 15 selected numbers are 1:1,048.

P6/6 = 0.33%   10 games

You can play either the following numbers or replace them with your favorite numbers:

LP+ Selection	Key #							
YOUR #'s	4	6	7	16	17	19	23	26

LP+ Selection							
YOUR #'s	28	29	33	34	36	38	39

1. 4 6 16 23 28 33
2. 4 6 16 26 28 36
3. 4 6 23 26 33 36
4. 4 7 17 19 34 38

5. 4 7 17 29 34 39
6. 4 7 19 29 38 39
7. 4 16 23 26 33 36

8. 4 17 19 29 38 39
9. 4 19 29 34 38 39
10. 4 23 26 28 33 36

CT, NY, TRI-STATE 6/40
*—A wheeling system that reduces the odds to **1:137,085***

System 17   THE 8 NUMBER COMBINATION

*First Prize (6 out of 6) is guaranteed if **all** 6 winning numbers are among the 8 selected numbers.*
The odds of having all 6 winning numbers among the 8 selected numbers are 1:137,085.

P6/6 = 100%   28 games

You can play either the following numbers or replace them with your favorite numbers:

LP+ Selection							
YOUR #'s	9	15	24	29	32	35	38	40

1. 9 15 24 29 32 35
2. 9 15 24 29 32 38
3. 9 15 24 29 32 40
4. 9 15 24 29 35 38
5. 9 15 24 29 35 40
6. 9 15 24 29 38 40
7. 9 15 24 32 35 38
8. 9 15 24 32 35 40
9. 9 15 24 32 38 40
10. 9 15 24 35 38 40

11. 9 15 29 32 35 38
12. 9 15 29 32 35 40
13. 9 15 29 32 38 40
14. 9 15 29 35 38 40
15. 9 15 32 35 38 40
16. 9 24 29 32 35 38
17. 9 24 29 32 35 40
18. 9 24 29 32 38 40
19. 9 24 29 35 38 40

20. 9 24 32 35 38 40
21. 9 29 32 35 38 40
22. 15 24 29 32 35 38
23. 15 24 29 32 35 40
24. 15 24 29 32 38 40
25. 15 24 29 35 38 40
26. 15 24 32 35 38 40
27. 15 29 32 35 38 40
28. 24 29 32 35 38 40

IL, NY, LOTTO AMERICA 6/54
*—A wheeling system that reduces the odds down to **1:1,391***

System 18   THE 18 NUMBER COMBINATION

*Third Prize (4 out of 6) is guaranteed if **all** 6 winning numbers are among the 18 selected numbers. The odds of having all 6 winning numbers among the 18 selected numbers are 1:1,391.*

P6/6 = 0.23%   42 games   **$21**

You can play either the following numbers or replace them with your favorite numbers:

LP+ Selection	2	5	9	16	20	23	26	30	33
YOUR #'s									

LP+ Selection	35	38	39	42	44	47	51	53	54
YOUR #'s									

1. 2 5 9 16 20 23	*15.* 5 16 26 39 42 54	*29.* 9 20 33 38 42 54
2. 2 5 9 26 30 33	*16.* 5 16 30 35 44 51	*30.* 9 23 26 35 47 54
3. 2 5 9 35 38 39	*17.* 5 16 33 38 47 53	*31.* 9 23 30 38 42 51
4. 2 5 9 42 44 47	*18.* 5 20 26 35 44 53	*32.* 9 23 33 39 44 53
5. 2 5 9 51 53 54	*19.* 5 20 30 38 47 54	*33.* 16 20 23 26 30 33
6. 2 16 26 35 42 51	*20.* 5 20 33 39 42 51	*34.* 16 20 23 35 38 39
7. 2 16 30 38 44 53	*21.* 5 23 26 38 47 51	*35.* 16 20 23 42 44 47
8. 2 16 33 39 47 54	*22.* 5 23 30 39 42 53	*36.* 16 20 23 51 53 54
9. 2 20 26 38 44 54	*23.* 5 23 33 35 44 54	*37.* 26 30 33 35 38 39
10. 2 20 30 39 47 51	*24.* 9 16 26 38 42 53	*38.* 26 30 33 42 44 47
11. 2 20 33 35 42 53	*25.* 9 16 30 39 44 54	*39.* 26 30 33 51 53 54
12. 2 23 26 39 47 53	*26.* 9 16 33 35 47 51	*40.* 35 38 39 42 44 47
13. 2 23 30 35 42 54	*27.* 9 20 26 39 44 51	*41.* 35 38 39 51 53 54
14. 2 23 33 38 44 51	*28.* 9 20 30 35 47 53	*42.* 42 44 47 51 53 54

MD, MI, MO, OH, OR, WA 6/44
*—A wheeling system that reduces the odds down to **1:380***

System 19   THE 18 NUMBER COMBINATION

Third Prize (4 out of 6) is guaranteed if 1 number from each Group is among the 6 winning numbers. The odds of having all 6 winning numbers among the 18 selected numbers are 1:380.

P6/6 = 2.5%   18 games   **$18**

You can play either the following numbers or replace them with your favorite numbers:

	GROUP 1			*GROUP 2*			*GROUP 3*		
LP+ Selection	15	25	35	16	26	36	17	27	37
YOUR #'s									

	GROUP 4			*GROUP 5*			*GROUP 6*		
LP+ Selection	18	28	38	19	29	39	20	30	40
YOUR #'s									

1.	15 16 17 18 29 20		*7.*	25 16 27 18 29 30		*13.*	35 16 17 38 29 40
2.	15 16 27 28 29 40		*8.*	25 16 37 38 29 20		*14.*	35 16 37 28 29 30
3.	15 26 27 38 39 30		*9.*	25 26 17 28 39 30		*15.*	35 26 17 18 39 40
4.	15 26 37 18 39 20		*10.*	25 26 37 38 39 40		*16.*	35 26 27 28 39 20
5.	15 36 17 38 19 30		*11.*	25 36 17 28 19 20		*17.*	35 36 27 38 19 20
6.	15 36 37 28 19 40		*12.*	25 36 27 18 19 40		*18.*	35 36 37 18 19 30

CO 6/42—*A wheeling system that reduces the odds to 1:1,048*

System 20   THE 15 NUMBER COMBINATION

Second Prize (5 out of 6) is guaranteed if 1 number from each Group is among the 6 winning numbers. The odds of having all 6 winning numbers among the 15 selected numbers are 1:1,048.

P6/6 = 11.1%   *24 games*

You can play either the following numbers or replace them with your favorite numbers:

	GROUP 1			GROUP 2			GROUP 3		
LP+ Selection	13	14	15	20	21	22	27	28	29
YOUR #'s									

	GROUP 4		GROUP 5		GROUP 6	
LP+ Selection	32	33	36	37	40	41
YOUR #'s						

1.	13 20 27 32 36 40		*9.*	14 21 28 32 36 40		*17.*	15 22 29 32 36 40
2.	13 22 28 32 36 41		*10.*	14 20 29 32 36 41		*18.*	15 21 27 32 36 41
3.	13 21 29 32 37 40		*11.*	14 22 27 32 37 40		*19.*	15 20 28 32 37 40
4.	13 21 29 32 37 41		*12.*	14 22 27 32 37 41		*20.*	15 20 28 32 37 41
5.	13 21 29 33 36 40		*13.*	14 22 27 33 36 40		*21.*	15 20 28 33 36 40
6.	13 21 29 33 36 41		*14.*	14 22 27 33 36 41		*22.*	15 20 28 33 36 41
7.	13 22 28 33 37 40		*15.*	14 20 29 33 37 40		*23.*	15 21 27 33 37 40
8.	13 20 27 33 37 41		*16.*	14 21 28 33 37 41		*24.*	15 22 29 33 37 41

Bet only in accordance with your means.

The Lotto ticket you receive from the retailer is the only evidence of your play.

For your own protection, be sure to complete the back of your ticket immediately after purchase.

PA 6/48—*A wheeling system that reduces the odds to 1:164*

System 21   THE 22 NUMBER COMBINATION

*Third Prize (4 out of 6) is guaranteed if **both** Key Numbers + any 4 numbers from the 22
selected numbers are among the 6 winning numbers. The odds of having all 6 winning numbers
among the 22 selected numbers are 1:164.*   *P6/6 = 0.2%*   *12 games*

You can play either the following numbers or replace them with your favorite numbers:

	Key #'s							
LP+ Selection	**21**	**38**	**1**	**6**	**8**	**9**	**11**	**12**	**16**
YOUR #'s								

LP+ Selection	**17**	**18**	**22**	**23**	**25**	**26**	**29**	**32**	**33**
YOUR #'s									

LP+ Selection	**35**	**36**	**39**	**40**
YOUR #'s				

1. 21 38 1 9 12 26	*5.* 21 38 6 11 23 40	*9.* 21 38 12 22 26 36
2. 21 38 1 9 22 36	*6.* 21 38 8 16 25 33	*10.* 21 38 16 17 25 35
3. 21 38 1 22 32 39	*7.* 21 38 8 17 33 35	*11.* 21 38 18 23 29 40
4. 21 38 6 11 18 29	*8.* 21 38 9 12 32 39	*12.* 21 38 26 32 36 39

IL 5/35—*A Pick 5 wheeling system that reduces the odds to 1:702*
FL 5/39—*A Pick 5 wheeling system that reduces the odds to 1:1,246*
RI 5/40—*A Pick 5 wheeling system that reduces the odds to 1:1,424*

System 22   THE 11 NUMBER COMBINATION

*Second Prize (5 out of 6) is guaranteed if any 5 numbers from the 11 selected numbers are among
the 5 winning numbers. The odds of having all 5 winning numbers among the 11 selected
numbers are 1:1,424.*   *P6/6 = 5.6%*   *26 games*

You can play either the following numbers or replace them with your favorite numbers:

LP+ Selection	**5**	**8**	**14**	**19**	**25**	**28**
YOUR #'s						

LP+ Selection	**33**	**34**	**37**	**39**	**40**
YOUR #'s					

1. 5 8 14 34 39	*10.* 5 28 33 37 40	*19.* 14 19 28 34 40
2. 5 8 19 25 34	*11.* 8 14 19 28 37	*20.* 14 19 33 34 37
3. 5 8 28 33 34	*12.* 8 14 19 33 40	*21.* 14 25 28 34 37
4. 5 8 34 37 40	*13.* 8 14 25 28 40	*22.* 14 25 33 34 40
5. 5 14 19 25 39	*14.* 8 14 25 33 37	*23.* 19 28 34 37 39
6. 5 14 28 33 39	*15.* 8 19 28 39 40	*24.* 19 33 34 39 40
7. 5 14 37 39 40	*16.* 8 19 33 37 39	*25.* 25 28 34 39 40
8. 5 19 25 28 33	*17.* 8 25 28 37 39	*26.* 25 33 34 37 39
9. 5 19 25 37 40	*18.* 8 25 33 39 40	

MD, MI, MO, OH, OR, WA 6/44—*A system that reduces the odds to 1:24*

System 23   THE 27 NUMBER COMBINATION

Third Prize (4 out of 6) is guaranteed if both Key Numbers + any 3 numbers from the 27 selected numbers are among the 6 winning numbers. The odds of having all 6 winning numbers among the 27 selected numbers are 1:24.   P6/6 = 0.1%   26 games

You can play either the following numbers or replace them with your favorite numbers:

		Key Number							
LP+ Selection	15	28	1	2	3	6	9	14	16
YOUR #'s									

LP+ Selection	18	19	20	21	26	27	29	30	32
YOUR #'s									

LP+ Selection	33	34	36	37	38	40	42	43	44
YOUR #'s									

1. 15 28 1 2 40 44
2. 15 28 1 3 9 26
3. 15 28 1 14 18 21
4. 15 28 1 30 33 34
5. 15 28 1 37 42 43
6. 15 28 2 6 16 29
7. 15 28 2 19 20 27
8. 15 28 2 32 36 38
9. 15 28 3 6 27 38

10. 15 28 3 14 30 37
11. 15 28 3 18 33 42
12. 15 28 3 21 34 43
13. 15 28 6 19 32 40
14. 15 28 6 20 36 44
15. 15 28 9 14 34 42
16. 15 28 9 18 30 43
17. 15 28 9 21 33 37
18. 15 28 14 16 20 32

19. 15 28 14 26 33 43
20. 15 28 16 19 38 44
21. 15 28 16 27 36 40
22. 15 28 18 19 29 36
23. 15 28 18 26 34 37
24. 15 28 20 29 38 40
25. 15 28 21 26 30 42
26. 15 28 27 29 32 44

D.C., DE, IO, MA, WV 6/36—*A wheeling system that reduces the odds to 1:4,216*

System 24   THE 11 NUMBER COMBINATION

Second Prize (5 out of 6) is guaranteed if any 6 numbers from the 11 selected numbers are among the 6 winning numbers. The odds of having all 6 winning numbers among the 11 selected numbers are 1:4,216.   P6/6 = 5.8%   27 games

You can play either the following numbers or replace them with your favorite numbers:

LP+ Selection	2	7	9	14	16	17	25	27	30	33	36
YOUR #'s											

1. 2 7 9 14 16 17
2. 2 7 9 14 30 36
3. 2 7 9 16 27 36
4. 2 7 9 17 27 30
5. 2 7 14 16 33 36
6. 2 7 14 17 30 33
7. 2 7 16 17 27 33
8. 2 7 27 30 33 36
9. 2 9 14 16 25 36

10. 2 9 14 17 25 30
11. 2 9 16 17 25 27
12. 2 9 25 27 30 36
13. 2 14 16 17 25 33
14. 2 14 25 30 33 36
15. 2 16 25 27 33 36
16. 2 17 25 27 30 33
17. 7 9 14 25 27 33
18. 7 9 16 25 30 33

19. 7 9 17 25 33 36
20. 7 14 16 25 27 30
21. 7 14 17 25 27 36
22. 7 16 17 25 30 36
23. 9 14 16 27 30 33
24. 9 14 17 27 33 36
25. 9 16 17 30 33 36
26. 14 16 17 27 30 36
27. 16 17 25 27 30 33

PA 7/11/80

System 25 **THE 9 NUMBER COMBINATION**

First Prize (7 out of 7) is guaranteed if any 7 numbers from the 9 selected numbers are among the 9 winning numbers. *P7/7 = 100%* *36 games*

You can play either the following numbers or replace them with your favorite numbers:

LP+ Selection	1	6	9	12	26	32	35	36	39
YOUR #'s									

1. 1 6 9 12 26 32 35	*13.* 1 6 9 26 32 36 39	*25.* 1 9 12 26 35 36 39
2. 1 6 9 12 26 32 36	*14.* 1 6 9 26 35 36 39	*26.* 1 9 12 32 35 36 39
3. 1 6 9 12 26 32 39	*15.* 1 6 9 32 35 36 39	*27.* 1 9 26 32 35 36 39
4. 1 6 9 12 26 35 36	*16.* 1 6 12 26 32 35 36	*28.* 1 12 26 32 35 36 39
5. 1 6 9 12 26 35 39	*17.* 1 6 12 26 32 35 39	*29.* 6 9 12 26 32 35 36
6. 1 6 9 12 26 36 39	*18.* 1 6 12 26 32 36 39	*30.* 6 9 12 26 32 35 39
7. 1 6 9 12 32 35 36	*19.* 1 6 12 26 35 36 39	*31.* 6 9 12 26 32 36 39
8. 1 6 9 12 32 35 39	*20.* 1 6 12 32 35 36 39	*32.* 6 9 12 26 35 36 39
9. 1 6 9 12 32 36 39	*21.* 1 6 26 32 35 36 39	*33.* 6 9 12 32 35 36 39
10. 1 6 9 12 35 36 39	*22.* 1 9 12 26 32 35 36	*34.* 6 9 26 32 35 36 39
11. 1 6 9 26 32 35 36	*23.* 1 9 12 26 32 35 39	*35.* 6 12 26 32 35 36 39
12. 1 6 9 26 32 35 39	*24.* 1 9 12 26 32 36 39	*36.* 9 12 26 32 35 36 39

Do you need a larger selection of Lotto Systems ?

If you need a larger selection of Basic Wheeling Systems with detailed Prize Guarantees, you can find over **60** of these systems in the book *The Only Way to Win at Lotto* by Robert Serotic (Second Edition, 1987), published by L.S.I. Publishing, Inc., 1259 El Camino Real, Suite 217, Menlo Park, CA 94025. This book will bring you over **80** very popular *Systems with Key Numbers* plus over **50 Lucky Bag Systems** (!) that will satisfy even the most "unlucky" players as well as those players with a low weekly Lotto budget! The book also introduces **71** Group Systems, Six-Group Systems, and Giants and Conditional Compound Systems suitable for Lotto Clubs and Family Pools.

Do you want to take advantage of playing these "error-free" systems?

EURO—LOTTOGRAF™ is your winning tool!

I created *EURO-LOTTOGRAF™* to make playing Lotto with number systems as fast and easy as possible. You already know the powerful advantages of using Number Systems, now you have a tool to make Number Systems a breeze to use. *EURO-LOTTOGRAF™* has an ingeniously designed Case plus different System Slides, which makes substituting your numbers into a number system as easy as 1-2-3. With the introductory package, you receive the *EURO-LOTTOGRAF™* Case plus Six Systems featuring 1 Pair and 5 Basic Systems (8, 9, 12, 14, and 18 Number Systems). Other System Slides will be made available in the future, making *EURO-LOTTOGRAF™* a tool you will never outgrow, and making Number Systems Super-Easy!

INTERNATIONAL LOTTERIES

The following pages provide you with descriptions of some of the most fruitful lotteries in the world. There are also lotteries which you can have access to by using your credit card and telephone. That information can be found in the Subscription Agencies section immediately following this section.

By reading about Australia's Lotto 6/45, the many games in Canada, and West Germany's lottery, you will receive a good cross section of the types of lotteries you can find. With this information you can stretch out beyond your borders and possibly win your fortunes the way we would most like to, in one lump sum.

EUROPE

The lottery in Europe is an old tradition. The first European record of lotteries, in which one could win a prize, was from 15th century Burgundy and Belgium. The first public lottery to have paid money as prizes is believed to be La Lotto de Firenze in Italy in 1530. Soon after, other Italian cities also began administrating their own lotteries. Since Benedetto Gentile founded the first Lotto Number game in Europe, Lotto di Genova in 1720, this type of game has become the most popular in lottery history. In 1863, *Lotto*, the first *national* lottery was created.

Today, lotteries are held in countries all over the world, but European lotteries still remain as the most popular. And then there are the unforgettable lotteries:

• Spain's *Loteria de Navidad*, established in 1763 by King Charles III to raise money for hospitals, features the world's largest Jackpot at $75 million.

• In 1751 Queen Maria Theresa of Austria started the first *Multi-state Lottery* for 5 countries: Austria, Bohemia & Moravia, Yugoslavia, Hungary & Slovakia and Italy. The game was called Lotto 5/90. The first official betting outlets were opened in Vienna and Graz (Austria), in Prague and Brun (Bohemia and Moravia — part of Czechoslovakia), in Pressburg (for Slovakia and Hungary), and in Trieste (for Italy and Yugoslavia).

Today, European lotteries run many different types of games, but Lotto and Toto-Pool are the most popular. Among many different Lotto games, Lotto 6/49 + Bonus is the most common. This game is played in Poland, Czechoslovakia, West Germany, Spain, etc. In many countries, Pick 5 Lotto is played. For example 5/35 in Poland and Czechoslovakia, 5/40 in Czechoslovakia, 5/90 in Hungary, Pick 5 in Italy, etc. In Scandinavia Pick 7 Lotto (7/35) is played. Although the lottery is very popular among European players, many countries do not build huge Jackpots, since the first prizes are limited. This allows payouts about three times larger than in the U.S. lotteries in the lower categories, because the unpaid money is transferred from the Jackpot category to the third, fourth and fifth category. On the other hand, Jackpots are paid in one lump-sum, mostly tax-free. And Europe has one rare lottery — in the Soviet Union lottery players compete for non-cash prizes.

European lotteries are joined in the oldest world lottery organization "INTERTOTO," which in the Tenth Congress of Intertoto in Rome, Italy, in 1985 represented 43 lotteries from Europe, Africa and America. The following table will show you what lottery games European players could enjoy at the time of thecongress:

	LOTTO GAMES	TOTO-POOL
Austria	1	1
Belgium	1	2
Bulgaria	1	1
Czechoslovakia	3	1+ Euro-Cup
Denmark	-	1
Finland	1	1
France	1	-
Greece	-	1
Hungary	1	1
Israel	-	1
Yugoslavia	1	1
Netherlands	2	2
Spain	1	1
Norway	-	1
East Germany	1	1
West Germany	2	2
Poland	4	2
Portugal	1	1
Romania	1	1
Switzerland	1	2
Sweden	1	2
Turkey	-	2
USSR	1	-

Many European lotteries also run other types of state lotteries, like for example the Red Cross Lottery, the State Instant Lotteries, the 3 Digit Lottery for the Blind, the Instant Lotteries for the Blind, the State Coupon Lotteries, the State Sweepstakes, the Christmas Lotteries, etc. But, Lotto and Toto-Pool are still the most popular games.

AUSTRALIA

Australia Lotto 6/45 is part of the Australian Lotto Bloc where six of Australia's seven states combine to run a national Lotto. Prizes are guaranteed by the six state governments.

Kind of Lotto	**Australian Lotto 6/45 + 2 Bonus Numbers**
How to Play	Select any **6** out of **45** numbers on **one** single board.
	For individuals residing in the United States, the game can be played by phone utilizing the I.L.A. subscription agency. This agency will provide you with special play forms. If you go to Australia or you are a resident, you can place your bet at any Lotto retailer using the official bet slips.
Price per Ticket	From 35¢ to 66¢ per game. The price per game depends on the number of games played and on the length of the betting period. The official price per one game differs from the price offered by any lottery subscription company, as these companies charge a "service commission."
Drawing	On national television every Saturday night at 9:30 pm. **Six** winning numbers are drawn from a field of **45** numbers. **Two** Bonus Numbers are drawn from the remaining **39** numbers.

Category	Match	Odds
Division 1	6 winning numbers	1:8,145,060
Division 2	any 5 winning numbers + either of Bonus Numbers	1:678,755
Division 3	any 5 winning numbers	1:36,689
Division 4	any 4 winning numbers	1:733
Division 5	any 4 winning numbers + either of Bonus Numbers	1:297

How the $ is Divided	Australian Lotto 6/45 is a pari-mutuel game and prizes are divided equally among winners in each prize category. From every dollar played, **60¢** is returned to players in the form of prizes.
Jackpot	The Jackpot (Division 1) is always over **$1.7** million. The Jackpot pool is **26.5%** of the share fund. All the prizes, including the Jackpot, are paid in one lump sum.
Lotto Subscription	Through the I.L.A. agency listed on page 64.
How to Claim a Prize	When played through the I.L.A. subscription agency — the company's computers check their entries for winnings. If you win under **$5,000**, you will receive a check by mail. If you win over **$5,000**, I.L.A. will notify you (and then you may decide to visit Australia to collect!).

CANADA

WESTERN CANADA

Manitoba Lotteries Foundation
830 Empress Street
Winnipeg, Manitoba
R3G 3H3
Telephone: (204) 945-2670

British Columbia
74 West Seymour Street
Kamloops,
British Columbia
V2C 1E2
Telephone: (604) 387-1011

Northwest Territories
Sport North
P.O.Box 504,
Yellowknife, Northwest Territories
X1A 1H0
Telephone: (403) 873-7723

Sask Sport Distributors, Inc.
1870 Lorne Street
Regina, Saskatchewan
S4P 2L7
Telephone: (306) 337-1414

Alberta
c/o Dep.of Consumers Affairs
11th Floor Capitol Square
10065 Jasper Avenue
Edmonton, Alberta
T5J 3B1
Telephone: (403) 427-3715

Yukon Lottery Commission
P.O.Box 5183
Whitehorse, Yukon
Y1A 5G2
Telephone: (403) 667-5915

ONTARIO

Ontario Lottery Corporation
2 Bloor Street West
Toronto, Ontario
M4W 3H8
Telephone: (416) 961-6262

ATLANTIC LOTTERY

Atlantic Lottery Corporation
770 St. George Boulevard
P.O. Box 5500
Moncton, N.B., E1C 8W6
Telephone: (506) 854-5680

QUEBEC

Loto Quebec
500, rue Sherbrooke Ouest
Montreal, Quebec
H3A 3G6
Telephone: (514) 873-5353

NATIONAL LOTTO 6/49 + BONUS

This is a multi-state game of all **10** Canadian states, administered by the Interprovincial Lottery Corporation. Although the game is run uniformly, the marketing and sales of tickets are provided by the Provincial Lottery Corporations listed on the previous page.

Kind of Lotto	Pick 6 Lotto — **Lotto 6/49 + Bonus Number**
Bet Slip	Six boards per bet slip.
How to Play	Select any 6 out of 49 numbers on one single board, and hand the bet slip to any Lotto retailer who will enter your bet slip into the On-Line Terminal that will print a Lotto 6/49 ticket with the numbers you have selected.
	For individuals residing in the United States, the game can be played by phone utilizing the services of a subscription agency. The agency will provide you with the special forms for playing.
Price per Ticket	**$1** per **one** game (board) per **one** drawing.
	The official price per one game differs from the price offered by any lottery subscription company, as these companies charge a "service commission."
Drawing	Live every Wednesday and Saturday at 11:20 p.m. **Six** winning numbers are drawn from a field of **49** numbers. **One** Bonus Number is drawn from the remaining **43** numbers.

Prize Category	Match	Odds
Jackpot (*6 out of 6*)	6 winning numbers	1:13,983,816
Second Prize (*5 out of 6+B*)	any 5 w. n. + Bonus Number	1:2,330,636
Third Prize (*5 out of 6*)	any 5 winning numbers	1:55,491
Fourth Prize (*4 out of 6*)	any 4 winning numbers	1:1,032
Fifth Prize (*3 out of 6*) (**$10**)	any 3 winning numbers	1:56

How the $ is Divided	Lotto 6/49 is a pari-mutuel game and prizes are divided equally among winners in each prize category. From every dollar played **45¢** is returned to players in the form of prizes.
How the Jackpot is Paid	The Jackpot is at least **$1** million (guaranteed). The Jackpot pool is **45%** of the share fund until the pool reaches **$7** million, and then **15%** after $7 million. All prizes are paid in one lump sum.
How to Claim a Prize	When played through a subscription agency, the agency will check your tickets and advise you of winnings;
	When played within Canada — you have **one** year to claim the prize.

LOTTERY SUBSCRIPTION SERVICES

A Lottery subscription service allows players the opportunity to play the on-line Lotto games in either their home state or another state or country without having to access an on-line Lotto retailer. Since federal law prohibits the transportation of Lottery tickets across state lines, it is important for the subscriber to understand how subscriptions are handled, and what to look for in a subscription service.

A subscription for Lotto is similar to a magazine or newspaper subscription, in that the subscriber receives a service for a pre-determined period of time. In this case, the service is playing the subscriber's numbers in a particular Lotto game. The fee for the service is included in the agency's price for a Lotto ticket (perhaps $1.60 for each $1.00 ticket). The fees differ with each subscription company. A higher number of tickets played normally reduces the fee charged per ticket.

Current postal regulations prohibit lottery transactions across state lines being conducted via the United States Postal Service. For this reason a reputable subscription service will conduct all of the transactions over the telephone and will usually charge the transaction to a major credit card.

Subscribers without a major credit card must realize that it will be necessary for them to ship payment for their subscription to the subscription service via United Parcel Service, Federal Express, or some other private delivery service and not via the United States Mail.

Since the actual Lotto tickets cannot cross state lines, a reliable subscription service should give the customer the option to receive some type of **Order Confirmation**. This confirmation should contain the numbers the customer is playing, the dates and games the numbers are being played in, and the price paid for the subscription. This is the customer's receipt for play and should not be sent in the mail. Confirmations are usually sent by way of United Parcel Service.

A very important part of the service provided by the subscription service is the notification of winners and assistance in collecting prizes. Subscribers should be given information as to where and how they can find out which numbers were drawn in each Lotto game, but it should be the subscription service's responsibility to determine which of it's customers win in each drawing. Subscription agencies utilize very powerful computer systems for all of the detailed functions they must perform so that a customer's order can be found and verified at the touch of a button. Customers should feel reassured to know that all of their numbers are being played and checked by the most modern computer systems available.

A reputable subscription service maintains confidential records. Customers should have confidence in the service, so that the fact they are playing a Lottery game (or when they win!) will not be revealed without the customer's permission.

IMPORTANT FACTORS TO UNDERSTAND IN USING SUBSCRIPTION SERVICES:

- Federal law **prohibits** sending Lottery tickets across state lines, and **Postal Regulations** prohibit lottery transactions via the United States Postal Service.

- It will not be possible to receive the actual Lotto tickets. The tickets are kept by the subscription agency in its files and the customer receives the confirmation of the numbers played.

- The subscription service will notify the players of any wins and will assist them in collecting their prizes.

- A **"service fee"** will be included in the price of the subscription and the subscriber will pay more than the actual cost of a Lotto ticket purchased in person at a Lotto retailer.

- A subscription service **is not** an official subscription agency of any State Lottery.

- The subscription agencies listed in this book are the U.S. and world leaders in this kind of service. All of them have an excellent reputation for their fast and efficient services.

- While the authors of this book recommend the subscription agencies listed in this book, the authors or L.S.I. Publishing, Inc., are not to be held responsible for the service of any subscription agency.

CANWIN   (CANADA)

✉	CANWIN P.O.Box 6100 • 349 West Georgia St. Vancouver B.C. V6B 4B5 Canada	☎	TOLL FREE 1-800-663-8781 Extension 7B02 *Order from anywhere in the U.S.A.*

☞ CANWIN has been marketing Canadian Lotteries including Lotto 6/49 in the U.S.A. for over 8 years and is a very reputable company. Canadian Lotteries have two distinct advantages over U.S. and many other world lotteries:

- *Lottery prizes are tax free in Canada*—The Canadian government does not take any tax-deductions on lottery winnings. When you win, you get a check for the full amount of your prize money.

- *Prizes are paid in lump sum*—this means that when you win, the payments are not spread out over years. You get all your money at once.

Lotto 6/49 Group Share Plan

Canadian Lotto 6/49 gives away jackpot prizes which can be as high as $15 million and more. There are hundreds of thousands of subsidiary prizes bringing the total prize pool up to as high as $28 million. Six winning numbers are drawn twice each week on Wednesday and Saturday.

Odds • Draws • Price • Winnings

- CANWIN's Group Share Plan shortens the odds by placing 250 players together in a group.
- Each group plays 84 computer selected sets of numbers for 30 draws (15 weeks) giving each group a total of 2,520 chances to win.
- The cost to each player in the group is US$29.95.
- The total prize money given away in 15 weeks is over $300 million!

STATE	Canada	*ODDS OF WINNING*	
LOTTO	6/49	**JACKPOT** — *6 out of 6*	1:13,983,816
SUBSCRIPTION		*5 out of 6 + Bonus Number*	1:2,330,636
CYCLE	30 draws	*5 out of 6*	1:55,491
PRICE	US$29.95/member	*4 out of 6*	1:1,032
DRAWING	Wed • Sat	*3 out of 6*	1:56

How To Enter

To enter the $29.95 Group Share Plan using Visa, MasterCard or Diners Club, call Toll Free 1-800-663-8781 and ask for extension 7B02.

- CANWIN will send you a confirmation of entry, including a list of all 84 sets of numbers for you and your group.
- After the final draw date, you will be sent a list of all the winning numbers for your draw dates, along with a check for the full amount of your winnings.
- All prizes are paid in one lump sum, tax free in Canada.
- CANWIN converts your winnings to U.S. dollars for your convenience.
- All players' names and information are confidential.

CROWN ROYAL   (CANADA)

| ✉ | CROWN ROYAL
Dept. 336 • 810 West Broadway
Vancouver B.C. V5Z 4C9 Canada | ☎ | TOLL FREE 1-800-663-8040
You can order from anywhere in
the U.S.A. (excluding Alaska) |

☞ CROWN ROYAL markets Canadian Lotto 6/49 to the U.S. and other foreign countries. As any other lottery subscription agency, CR charges a fee for its services, which is included in all prices quoted. Tickets are issued with 6 games for as many draws as you wish. All orders are filled within one working day of being received.

• **Super 8 wheels 8 numbers**

• **Club Royal wheels 9 numbers** for 3 draws for groups of 10 (252 chances to win). (Participating players get 1/10th of winnings)

Have your numbers from 1 to 49 ready and your Visa or MasterCard handy.

STATE	LOTTO	ODDS	SUBSCRIPTION CYCLE		DRAWING
Canada	6/49	1:13,983,816	2, 5, 10 draws	$26, $56, $100	Wed • Sa
			Super 8	$49	Wed • Sa
Prices quoted are in U.S. dollars			Club Royal	$54	Wed • Sa

All players are sent confirmation of play and winning numbers for games played, plus instructions how to collect winnings. All prizes are paid in one lump sum, tax free in Canada. Crown Royal converts your winnings to U.S. dollars for your convenience. Payment is sent according to your instructions. All players' names and information are confidential. CROWN ROYAL offers all of its players money saving specials several times a year.

UNIVERSAL INC.   (U.S.A.)

| ✉ | UNIVERSAL INC
4136 North State Road 7
Lauderdale Lakes • Florida 33319 | ☎ | TOLL FREE 1-800-729-3165
You can order from anywhere
in the U.S.A. |

☞ UNIVERSAL INC. acts as your agent in all ticket transactions, maintenance of records and reports. Service fees are included in all published costs. Upon receipt of the subscriber's number selection, ticket plays and credit card information, the data is entered into Universal's computer. The company offers the following subscribtion services:

• **Florida's Lotto 6/49 and Fanatsy 5**

• **6/49 and Fantasy 5 Pools** for groups of 25 players at a cost of $85 per share, which allows a total of 600 tickets to be played in that pool. Each pool plays for five draws in a row, each time playing 120 tickets (600 tickets over 5 draws).

STATE	LOTTO	ODDS	SUBSCRIPTION CYCLE		DRAWING
Florida	6/49	1:13,983,816	12, 24, 36 draws	1-10 tickets	Saturday
Florida	Fantasy 5	1:575,757	12, 24, 36 draws	1-10 tickets	Tu • Fri
special for both games—50 tickets per 1 draw					

Our computers process each order, keep track of the numbers and games being played and continuously search for possible winners among our subscribers. Federal regulations prohibit sending lottery tickets through the mail or across state lines. For this reason Universal Inc. will send all subscribers a confirmation letter showing your numbers played and play dates. The tickets are held by Universal Inc. in the subscriber's name. When picking numbers, you can provide us with your selection or let Universal's computer pick them for you.

FORTUNES UNLIMITED   (CANADA)

| ✉ | FORTUNES UNLIMITED
55 Mc Caul Street • Suite 3
Toronto M5T 2W7 Canada | ☎ | TOLL FREE   1-800-387-6028
Order from anywhere in the U.S.A. |

☞ **All Canadian Lottery prizes are paid in one tax-free lump sum amount.**

FORTUNES UNLIMITED is going into its third year of serving Americans who play Canadian lotteries. This is a full service agency that provides same day service so your numbers are entered right away, follow-up renewal reminders and monthly newsletters to keep you up to date on winning numbers and other lottery information. Also, you never miss a win because your plays are computer checked for wins. Wins are automatically sent out to you each week.

Lotto 6/49

Lotto 6/49 is Canada's biggest Jackpot lottery. It features a guaranteed minimum Jackpot of $1 million that grows until it's won. Match all 6 regular winning numbers to win the Jackpot. Subsidiary prizes are also available. Draws are held every Wednesday and Saturday. The record single Jackpot paid over $14 million!

If you match, in any order:	You win
All 6 winning numbers	Jackpot prize (min. $1 Million)
Any 5 winning numbers plus the Bonus Number	2nd prize
Any 5 winning numbers	3rd prize
Any 4 winning numbers	4th prize
Any 3 winning numbers	5th prize ($10)

How To Play

• Pick any 6 numbers from 1 to 49 for each game.
• You will receive an "Official Confirmation" of your entry including the numbers you are playing and the dates they are being played.
• Your numbers will be entered for 12 consecutive drawings.
• Your numbers can be picked by computer at no extra charge.

Cost

Fortunes Unlimited offers very competitive prices:
• The cost to play 1 game is $24, 2 games $46, 3 games $68, 6 games $120.
  (Only $1.67 per ticket when you play six games)
• Prices quoted are in U.S. dollars.
• All games will be played for 12 drawings.

How To Enter

To order by phone: call toll-free 1-800-387-6028. Have your credit card ready as well as the number of games you wish to play and the numbers you have picked for each game.

To order by mail: send in your numbers along with your name, address, telephone number and payment of your order to the address listed above. Payments can be made by check, money order, cash, Visa, MasterCard or American Express. If paying by credit card, please indicate your card number and expiration date.

Special Services

Fortunes Unlimited also specializes in other Canadian lotteries and longer subscriptions. You will receive a full information package with your first order. You are welcome to call their toll-free number for more information.

GAMING-PA   (USA)

✉ | GAMING-PA
P.O.Box 193
Wyano • PA 15695

☎ | 1-800-445-6886 (outside PA)
1-800-843-9498 (in Pennsylvania)
1-412-751-1540 (in Canada)

☞ GAMING-PA is a company founded with the objective of marketing the lotteries in Pennsylvania, Maryland, Missouri, New York, Ohio, West Virginia, and other states, in addition to non-domestic lotteries. GAMING-PA, as any other lottery subscription agency, charges a fee for its services which is included in all prices quoted in its literature. The following lottery games are provided by phone*:

Lotto Games

STATE	TYPE OF LOTTO	ODDS	SUBSCRIPTION CYCLE (weeks)	DRAWING
Canada	6/49	1:13,983,816	8, 16, 26	Sa
Florida	6/49	1:13,983,816	8, 16, 26	Sa
Germany	6/49	1:13,983,816	8, 16, 26	Sa
Lotto America	6/54	1:12,913,583*	8, 16, 26	Wed • Sa
Pennsylvania	6/48	1:6,135,756	8, 14, 26	Tu • Fri
Pennsylvania	7/11/80	1:9,626,413	8, 14, 26	Wed
Maryland	6/44	1:7,059,052	8, 16, 26	Sa
New York	6/40	1:3,838,380	8, 16, 26	Mo
New York	6/54	1:12,913,583*	8, 16, 26	Wed • Sa
New York	10/20/80	1:8,911,711	8, 16, 26	Daily Game
Missouri	6/44	1:7,059,052	8, 16, 26	Wed • Sa
Ohio	6/44	1:7,059,052	8, 16, 26	Wed
West Virginia	6/36	1:1,947,792	8, 16, 26	Wed

*per two plays (tickets)

Daily Games

GAMING-PA offers the Daily Pick-4 games in the following states:
Pennsylvania • Maryland • New York • Ohio • West Virginia

How to play

How to Enter You have to play by phone. Have your favorite numbers and the state you want to play selected before you call. The operator can explain the different plans in detail if you would like more information. Or, you can write to the company using the address above. After your order is completed, GAMING-PA will send you a "Confirmation Certificate" with a detailed schedule.

Winnings All games played are checked for winnings by the company's computer. You don't need to claim your winnings — GAMING-PA will take care of it.

How am I paid? Every state msy have different rules about how winnings are paid. Details for each lottery are explained in the section entitled **STATE LOTTERIES**.

GEHLE (WEST GERMANY)

✉ GEHLE • State Licensed Lottery Agent
Rheinallee 7
6500 Mainz • West Germany

☎ West Germany (0)40-511-7677

☞ GEHLE is the State Licensed Lottery Agent marketing the famous SOUTH GERMAN STATE LOTTERY. On November 18, 1989, this lottery will launch the biggest game ever—the prizes will reach over $243 million. There will be 1,000,000 ticket numbers issued with 478,857 chances to win, which makes almost every second ticket a winner. The top prizes are now 2 Jackpots, each paying $2.16 million plus four secondary Jackpots paying $1.62 million and $1.08! ...plus
• **18** prizes of $540,540 each, ...plus
• **thousands** of prizes worth up to $270,270.
All prizes are guaranteed by the German Government.

Three Steps To Start Playing

Step 1. Order any tickets listed in the following table:

STATE	DM	US $
1/1 ticket	894.00	484.00
1/2 ticket	462.00	250.00
1/4 ticket	246.00	133.00
5/4 COMBI	1,110.00	600.00

Step 2. Include payment with your order or pay after receiving your statement of account by personal cheque, bank transfer or money order. Or you can use your credit card (Visa, MasterCard). Don't forget to include expiration date.
Step 3. Within days you'll receive your ticket and all the relevant rules and regulations.

Checking for winners

86th lottery of the "Suddeutsche Klassenlotterie" will begin on November 18, 1989. Prices cover all 6 classes and include charges for shipping, postage and the official winning lists. There are no additional charges. Handling charge for payment by credit card is 6% (max. DM 45.00). Prices in US dollars are variable due to changes in the rate of exchange ($1.00=DM 1.85).

LOTTO POOLS AND LOTTO CLUBS

pages 76-78

Playing in Lotto Clubs or Family Pools can save you money.
Don't gamble!
Share The Lotto Expense— Share WINNINGS!

I.L.A. (AUSTRALIA)

✉ | I.L.A.
9 Ouyan Street
Bundall • Qld. 4217 • Australia

☎ | TOLL FREE   1-800-CASH-WIN
702-795-2399 (in Nevada)
Order from anywhere in the U.S.A.

Direct Correspondence to:
P.O.Box 5649 • Gold Coast Mail Centre • Qld. 4217 • Australia

☞ I.L.A.(International Lottery Agents) is a company founded by Mr. Terry E. Morris in 1984, with the objective of marketing Australian Lotteries to non-resident Australians. It provides contestants with information and computerized results. I.L.A., as any other lottery subscription agency, charges a fee for its services which is included in all prices quoted in its literature.

Lotto 6/45 + 2 Bonus Numbers

Australia Lotto 6/45 + 2 Bonus Numbers is part of the Australia Lotto Bloc where 6 of 7 states combine to run a National Lotto.

The Australian Lotto has a total field of 45 numbers. Six winning numbers are randomly drawn from the field of 45 numbers. Two Bonus Numbers are drawn from the remaining 39 numbers.

The numbers are drawn on Australian national television every Saturday at 8:30 pm.

Category	Match	Prize Pool %
Division 1	6 winning numbers (Jackpot)	26.0%
Division 2	any 5 winning numbers + either Bonus Number	7.5%
Division 3	any 5 winning numbers	13.5%
Division 4	any 4 winning numbers	23.5%
Division 5	any 3 winning numbers + either Bonus Number	29.0%

How Do I Play?

Australian Lotto uses Basic Wheeling Systems from 7 to 11 numbers (in Australia called "Permutation Systems") that can be found in my books "*The Only Way to Win at Lotto*" and "*Lotto: How To Play And Win— Introduction to Systems and Strategies.*" These systems are programed into the company's computer for instant substitution of your numbers. You can play from 7 to 462 games every week for 10, 20, 30 or even 50 consecutive drawings. And your entry costs only 35¢ to 66¢ per game.

How to Enter   Order the play board by phone or by mail using the above address or phone number. Select "Permutation System" and mark your favorite numbers. Return the completed board to I.L.A. with your entry fee. You will receive an "Entry Confirmation Certificate" and a detailed schedule.

Results   Every five weeks you receive your own computer print-out showing the previous ten weeks' results.

Winnings   All games played are checked for winnings by the company's computer. You don't need to claim your winnings – I.L.A. will take care of it.

How am I paid?   All prizes are paid in one lump sum.

LOTTERY PLAYERS OF AMERICA (U.S.A.)

| ✉ | LOTTERY PLAYERS OF AMERICA, INC.
1255 W. Broad Street
Stratford • CT 06497 | ☎ | 1-203-377-1410
Toll-Free Order Phones
Available To Members Only |

☞ Lottery Players of America, Inc. was founded to be both a club for lottery players and a commercial lottery subscription service.

LPA offers the opportunity to play the lotteries of New York, California, Illinois, Florida, Massachusetts, Connecticut, Pennsylvania, and Lotto America. Members can place their subscription by calling a toll free number. All members also can enter lotteries on a non-subscription basis with 72 hour notice to get into the "Big Jackpot." All members receive free confirmation of their play orders by United Parcel Service.

EVERY MEMBER OF THE CLUB RECEIVES

- A quarterly newsletter
- $50 in discounts for future lottery subscription purchases
- An exclusive 64-page book "Playing and Winning U.S. Lotteries"
- A membership book of information and playsheets
- Discounts on specially selected merchandise
- A *FREE* play in the New York Lotto 6/54 game.

Order on the ***Demonstration Line*** (interactive with touchtone phones) 1-900-860-9197 ($2 first minute, $1 each additional minute—partially refundable with membership).

LOTTO SYSTEMS TECHNOLOGIES (U.S.A.)

| ✉ | LOTTO SYSTEMS TECHNOLOGIES
270 North Cannon Dr. • Suite 649-539
Beverly Hills • CA 90210 | ☎ | Call TOLL-FREE
1-800-U-POOL-ME
1-800-876-6563
Info: 213-470-1839 |

☞ **LOTTO SYSTEMS TECHNOLOGIES** (LST™) offers services to Lotto players that like to play wheeling systems with a larger group of players (50) to reduce the cost. The company also offers wheeling systems to players who like to play their own numbers.

The compnay offers the opportunity to play two of the world's most popular Lotto games—California 6/49 and Florida Fantasy 5. The objective of the company is to market a wheeling system play. Members (18 and over) can place their subscription play by calling a toll free number. The contestants can also subscribe by sending a check or money order by UPS or Federal Express.

Lotto Systems Technologies offer 2 different services:

1. Playing in *California 6/49 Gold Mine Pool* and in *Florida Fantasy 5 Stars Pool*
   - 1 month/8 draws/$40—**single pool**
   - 1 month/8 draws/$80—**reverse pool**
   - 1 month/8 draws/$50—**FL single pool**
   - 1 month/16 draws/$90—**FL+CA pools**
2. Playing any wheeling system (with own number selection) offered by the company.

All members receive free confirmation of their play orders by United Parcel Service.

EVERY MEMBER OF THE CLUB RECEIVES

- A bi-monthly newsletter
- A $10 entry discount with the "reverse pool" subscription purchase
- A 10% discount on every product listed in the Lotto Catalog
- Free information about the club's results and winnings (1-213-470-1839)

U.S. LOTTERY GROUP (USA)

✉ U.S. LOTTERY GROUP Monticello Communications, Inc. 315 W. Livingston St. Monticello, IL 61856	☎ 1-800-372-9464 (1-800-DRAWING) 1-217-762-3521 (office) 1-217-762-9914 (fax)

☞ U.S. Lottery Group, a division of Monticello Communications Inc. (Monticello, Illinois), is a subscription agency that telemarkets Illinois, New York, Florida, California and Pennsylvania lotto games. The parent corporation, Monticello Communications, is a state-licensed Illinois lottery agent (#323220, dated July 1, 1983). Like other subscription services, USLG charges a fee for its services, which is included in all prices quoted in their literature. USLG does not charge any commission or fee against a player's winnings: players receive the entire prize amount to which they are entitled.

USLG is an Associate Member of the National Lottery Players Association.

The following lottery games are provided by phone*:

Subscriptions offered

STATE	TYPE OF LOTTO	ODDS (*per 2 plays)	SUBSCRIPTION CYCLE (weeks)	DRAWING
Illinois	6/54	1:12,913,583*	15, 26, 52	1 drawing/week (Sa)
Illinois	5/35	1324,632	15, 26, 52	3 drawings/week (Mo•Wed•Sa)
Pennsylvania	7/11/80	1:9,626,413	15, 26, 52	1 drawing/week (Wed)
New York	6/54	1:12,913,583*	15, 26, 52	2 drawings/week (Wed•Sa)
California	6/49	1:13,983,816	15, 26, 52	2 drawings/week (Wed•Sa)
Florida	6/49	1:13,983,816	15, 26, 52	1 drawing/week (Sa)
Florida	5/39	1:575,757	15, 26, 52	2 drawings/week (Tu•Fri)

Subscription cycles run for 15, 26 or 52 drawings. USLG also offers one-draws for these games. Customers may order tickets for a single drawing instead of a full subscription cycle, but a minimum-purchase condition and deadline may apply. A USLG operator has details.

How to play

How to Enter   Customers must play by telephone and pay by credit card. Call a USLG operator at the toll-free number (1-800-372-9464) and specify the game or games you want to play. Tell the operator which numbers you wish to play and which subscription cycle you wish to play. USLG will send a confirmation of your order via a private parcel carrier service.

Winnings   All games played through USLG are checked for winners by the company's high-speed computer. Also, customers receive the free weekly USLG newsletter, which lists weekly drawing results and winnings.

How am I paid?   Any winnings small enough to be paid out by a lotto retailer are paid in full within 7 to 10 days by USLG. For larger winnings, winners need not file a claim form with the state lottery. USLG files any paperwork on behalf of, and in the name of, the winner. For these prizes, every state may have different rules about payment. For more information, see the section of this book entitled STATE LOTTERIES.

GROUP PLAY   USLG offers customers two group play options, one for each Illinois lotto game. The detailed description can be found in the section "Lotto Pools & Clubs."

LOTTERY POOLS & CLUBS

GOLD LOTTO ONE (USA)

✉ U.S. LOTTERY GROUP
Monticello Communications, Inc.
315 W. Livingston St.
Monticello, IL 61856

☎ 1-800-372-9464 (1-800-DRAWING)
1-217-762-3521 (office)
1-217-762-9914 (fax)

☞ **Gold Lotto-One**

- This club plays a system that is computer-generated from 22 of the more frequently picked numbers in the weekly Illinois lotto 6/54 drawing.
- The system covers 74,632 combinations for each drawing.
- The combinations are divided among 982 subscriptions that each play 76 games per week.
- When all six winning numbers drawn are among the numbers wheeled by Gold Lotto-One, the odds of winning the grand prize are 1:982 per subscription over a year's play.
- Subscriptions may be purchased by a single player or by a "trustee" purchasing the subscription on behalf of a partnership.

Also, customers may purchase half- or quarter-ownership of a subscription.

To join Gold Lotto-One, call toll-free 1-800-372-9464 (1-800-DRAWING).

Players must be at least 18 years old, and must pay with their Visa, MasterCard or Discover credit card. Customers tell the operator that they want to buy a Lotto-One subscription, and provide their name, address, credit card number and card expiration date. The operator selects a subscription from the computer in which the player may buy the following ownership options:

Subscriptions offered

1 DRAW/WEEK	100% Ownership	50% Ownership	25% Ownership
1 yr. (52 draws)	$2,600	$1,300	$650
1/2 yr. (26 draws)	$1,300	$650	$325
3 mos. (16 draws)	$650	$325	$165
6 wks. (6 draws)	$400	$200	$100

The player receives an official confirmation of membership in Gold Lotto-One via a private parcel carrier service.

GOLD LOTTO CASH 5 (USA)

| ✉ | U.S. LOTTERY GROUP
Monticello Communications, Inc.
315 W. Livingston St.
Monticello, IL 61856 | ☎ | 1-800-372-9464 (1-800-DRAWING)
1-217-762-3521 (office)
1-217-762-9914 (fax) |

☞ Gold Lotto Cash 5

- This club plays a system, or "wheel," that is computer-generated from 25 of the more frequently picked numbers in the Illinois 5/35 Little Lotto-Cash 5 game.
- There are three Cash 5 drawings a week.
- The system covers every possible combination of those 25 numbers—53,125 combinations in all—for each drawing.
- The combinations are divided among 2,125 subscriptions that each play 25 games per drawing.
- When all five winning numbers drawn are among the numbers wheeled by Gold Lotto Cash 5, the odds of winning the grand prize are 1:2,125 per subscription if it is played three times a week over a year.
- Subscriptions may be purchased by a single player or by a "trustee" purchasing the subscription on behalf of a partnership. Also, customers may purchase half- or quarter-ownership of a subscription.

To join Gold Lotto Cash 5, call toll-free 1-800-372-9464 (1-800-DRAWING). Players must be at least 18 years old, and must pay with their Visa, MasterCard or Discover credit card. Customers tell the operator that they want to buy a Gold Lotto Cash 5 subscription, and provide their name, address, credit card number and card expiration date. The operator selects a subscription from the computer in which the player may buy the following ownership options:

Subscriptions offered

3 DRAWS/WEEK	100% Ownership	50% Ownership	25% Ownership
1 yr. (156 draws)	$4,500	$2,250	$1,125
1/2 yr. (78 draws)	$2,425	$1,225	$625
3 mos. (39 draws)	$1,325	$675	$350
4 wks. (12 draws)	$550	$275	$150

1 DRAW/WEEK	100% Ownership	50% Ownership	25% Ownership
1 yr. (52 draws)	$1,775	$900	$450
1/2 yr. (26 draws)	$1,000	$500	$250
3 mos. (13 draws)	$550	$275	$150
4 wks. (4 draws)	$200	$100	$50

The player receives an official confirmation of membership in Gold Lotto Cash 5 via a private parcel carrier service.

FANTASY 5 STARS & CA 6/49 GOLD MINE POOLS (USA)

✉ LOTTO SYSTEMS TECHNOLOGIES
270 North Canon Dr.   Suite 649-539
Beverly Hills, CA 90210

☎ 1-800-U-POOL-ME (orders)
1-800-876-6563 (orders)
1-213-470-1839 (information)

☞ FLORIDA FANTASY 5 STARS POOL

- This sophisticated pool uses the best 16 number wheeling system ever developed. The system was tested by the computer software Lottery Dollars and its probability of winning the Jackpot is 3.4% with five numbers right!!
- Lotto Edge's in-house powerful computers analyze all drawings and choose a balanced selection of 16 numbers in the Florida Fantasy 5/39 Lotto that pays all winnings in cash as one lump-sum. But, players must be at least 18 years old!
- There are two Fantasy 5 drawings a week (Tuesday and Friday).
- Every pool contestant participates in 8 drawings a month and has 1,184 chances to win for as low as $50 per 8 drawings!
- When all five winning numbers drawn are among the numbers wheeled by the Fantasy 5 Stars Pool, the odds of winning the Jackpot are 1:29!

To join **Fantasy 5 Stars Pool**, call toll-free 1-800-U-POOL-ME (1-800-876-6563). The subscription program is introduced on the bottom of this page.

☞ CALIFORNIA 6/49 GOLD MINE POOL

- The most powerful California pool uses an exciting "over-lap" wheeling system for 18 numbers, reducing the odds of having all 6 numbers in the group of 18 from 1:14 million to 1:753 (!!) and is comprised of twenty groups (sub-pools) of 9 and 18 number wheels.
- Lotto Edge's in-house powerful computers analyze all drawings and select a balanced selection of 18 numbers.
- There are two California 6/49 drawings a week (Wednesday and Saturday).
- Every pool contestant participates in a single pool (8 drawings) and has 1,008 chances to win, or plays in a reverse sub-pool and has 2,016 chances to win.
- Purchasing a **"reverse sub-pool"** subscription is the smartest way of playing. When the pool hits all six winning numbers and they are not hit by one sub-pool, a player automatically **wins a Jackpot** in the reverse sub-pool, plus 18 "5 out of 6"... plus 45 "4 out of 6"...plus more!!!

To join **6/49 Gold Mine Pool**, call toll-free 1-800-U-POOL-ME (1-800-876-6563). The subscription program is introduced on the bottom of this page.

Subscription Offered 1 share ownership	CA 6/49 Gold Mine	FL Fantasy 5 Stars Pool	Both Pools—Gold Mine & Stars Pool
8 draws	$40	$50	$90
8 draws/reverse pools	$80	N/A	$130
24 draws	$115	$145	$255
24 draws/reverse pools	$215	N/A	$360
48 draws	$220	$280	$490
48 draws/reverse pools	$420	N/A	$700

The player receives an official confirmation of membership in both pools via a private parcel carrier service (UPS, Federal Express or FAX).

WHEELING SYSTEMS
• DEVELOPMENT •
• SERVICES •

Custom Wheel Network™
Computer Generated Systems
Custom Wheeling Systems

Custom Wheel Network NLPA
L.S.I. Publishing Inc.
1259 El Camino Real • Suite 217
Menlo Park • CA 94025

Telephone:
1-800-526-8899 (outside CA)
1-408-980-1999 (in CA)
1-408-980-5174 (consult. services)

Custom Wheel Network (CWN) is service for lotto players, lotto clubs and pools. In addition to the custom wheeling systems developed by Robert Serotic, CWN now offers "Computer Generated Systems" using the latest Lotto computer technology. This means that a player can choose from the widest range of wheeling systems ever developed (see the listings on the following pages).

Computer Generated Systems are available for any Pick 6, 5 and 7 Lotto games worldwide and will be developed according to player's budget, prize guarantee and type of lotto you play.

The development charge of Computer Generated Systems is only 10¢-$1 per game (example: an 80 game system based on 25¢/1game = $20). A player can obtain either a model wheeling system (using the standard 01 02 03...format) or if you provide Custom Wheel Network with your lucky numbers, CWN can generate the system with the games ready to be copied into bet slips (please, write your number selection on a separate sheet).

Most systems are completed between seven to ten days and are sent to you according to your instructions (Over Night Delivery or Priority Mail, etc.). Please include $3 for shipping/handling, $13 for overnight delivery.

For those of you who use a PC compatible computer, you can receive your wheeling system on a 5.25" floppy disk with a special operating program allowing you to replace your own numbers into the system easily and as often as you like. This special custom diskette costs only $24.95 in addition to the cost of the custom system.

On the next page you will find the complete list of computer generated systems. Each system shows the prize guarantee, the amount of games played and the cost of development.

Custom Wheel Network

lotto number system development

L.S.I. Publishing

Quality Product

Custom Wheel Network • 1259 El Camino Real • Menlo Park • CA 94025 • 1-408-980-1999 (CA) • 1-800-526-8899 (USA)

Pick 6 Lotto

#'s Played	Prize Guar.	Games Played	Development Cost
25#	3/6	78	$16
26#	3/6	80	$16
27#	3/6	86	$17
28#	3/6	91	$18
29#	3/6	94	$19
30#	3/6	115	$23
31#	3/6	125	$25
32#	3/6	131	$27
33#	3/6	139	$28
34#	3/6	152	$31
35#	3/6	164	$41
36#	3/6	184	$46
37#	3/6	199	$50
38#	3/6	221	$54
39#	3/6	244	$61
40#	3/6	275	$69
42#	3/6	307	$80
44#	3/6	355	$100
45#	3/6	380	$125
46#	3/6	411	$165
49#	3/6	496	$200
54#	3/6	672	$240
20#	4/6	154	$31
21#	4/6	196	$41
22#	4/6	248	$46
23#	4/6	299	$50
24#	4/6	367	$54
25#	4/6	434	$61
26#	4/6	520	$69
27#	4/6	623	$80
28#	4/6	734	$100
29#	4/6	853	$125
30#	4/6	1005	$165
31#	4/6	1163	$200
32#	4/6	1331	$240
33#	4/6	1528	$280
34#	4/6	1737	$320
35#	4/6	1973	$345
36#	4/6	2240	$370
37#	4/6	2539	$390
38#	4/6	2836	$400
13#	5/6	116	$55
14#	5/6	203	$80
15#	5/6	315	$105
16#	5/6	504	$180
17#	5/6	588	$195
18#	5/6	756	$220
19#	5/6	988	$240
20#	5/6	1305	$270
23#	5/6	3224	$650
24#	5/6	4316	$800

Note: The prizes are 100% guaranteed when all six winning numbers are among the group of numbers played.

Pick 5 Lotto

#'s Played	Prize Guar.	Games Played	Development Cost
10#	3/5	6	$6
11#	3/5	6	$6
12#	3/5	12	$10
13#	3/5	12	$10
14#	3/5	13	$10
15#	3/5	27	$18
16#	3/5	35	$22
17#	3/5	47	$26
18#	3/5	51	$27
19#	3/5	59	$30
20#	3/5	71	$33
25#	3/5	148	$48
30#	3/5	271	$80
35#	3/5	456	$96
39#	3/5	636	$135
40#	3/5	694	$148
8#	4/5	7	$7
9#	4/5	14	$12
10#	4/5	22	$17
11#	4/5	34	$25
12#	4/5	54	$30
13#	4/5	87	$35
14#	4/5	127	$40
15#	4/5	189	$44
16#	4/5	273	$64
17#	4/5	308	$75
18#	4/5	364	$109
19#	4/5	444	$113
20#	4/5	552	$120
21#	4/5	693	$135
22#	4/5	873	$160
23#	4/5	1099	$180
24#	4/5	1379	$210
25#	4/5	1722	$233
26#	4/5	2098	$258
27#	4/5	2550	$284
28#	4/5	3090	$322
29#	4/5	3731	$380
30#	4/5	4459	$446

Note: The prizes are 100% guaranteed when all five winning numbers are among the group of numbers played.

Acknowledgment

Custom Wheel Network™ thanks Gary Olander, author of the exciting IBM programs "Let's Make A Wheel" and "Probaloto," for his great effort and achievment in the developing the Computer Generated Systems Network.
Computer Generated Systems were developed on high speed 386 IBM computers! All systems are perfectly balanced and the authors guarantee that no "typo" or "missprint" can occur. These systems will always bring the guaranteed prize 100% of the time.   *Robert Serotic*

Pick 7 Lotto

#'s Played	Prize Guar.	Games Played	Development Cost
10#	5/7	3	$3
11#	5/7	5	$5
12#	5/7	11	$11
13#	5/7	18	$15
14#	5/7	27	$20
15#	5/7	43	$30
16#	5/7	63	$40
17#	5/7	105	$48
18#	5/7	154	$58
19#	5/7	214	$65
20#	5/7	280	$70
21#	5/7	372	$80
22#	5/7	492	$95
23#	5/7	640	$125
24#	5/7	816	$160
25#	5/7	1023	$190
26#	5/7	1296	$210
27#	5/7	1610	$232
28#	5/7	1992	$265
29#	5/7	2428	$295
10#	6/7	10	$10
11#	6/7	26	$18
12#	6/7	54	$30
13#	6/7	116	$48
14#	6/7	232	$65
15#	6/7	435	$80
16#	6/7	715	$130
17#	6/7	904	$160
18#	6/7	1242	$210
19#	6/7	1796	$285
20#	6/7	2608	$390

Note: The prizes are 100% guaranteed when all seven winning numbers are among the group of numbers played.

Custom Wheel Network

lotto number system development

L.S.I. Publishing

Quality Product

Custom Wheel Network • 1259 El Camino Real • Menlo Park • CA 94025 • 1-408-980-1999 (CA) • 1-800-526-8899 (USA)

Custom Made Wheels

If you are interested in obtaining a lotto number wheel developed by Robert Serotic's Custom Wheel Network for you/your company/LottoClub/Family Pool, this service is for you. Custom Wheel Network is the world's unique laboratory, which can develop any type of Lotto Number System (also called Wheeling Systems or just Wheels) based on your needs and specifications. Robert Serotic offers two different programs:

1. A development of Wheeling Systems ("WS") for single players and private lottery groups (non-profit pools and clubs). "WS" are not intended to be used by commercial lottery organizations, subscription agencie or professional pools. For the service of developing a custom "WS," depending on the complexity of the system, Custom Wheel Network will charge between 25¢ to $1 per game of the system.

2. A development of "WS" for commercial lottery organizations, subscription agencies or professional pools. Wheeling Systems will be developed on a royalty basis of either 10% from Gross Receipts or 33% from Net Receipts realized from sales. In some cases a "WS" can be paid off lump-sum.

   Please, indicate which royalty arrangement is agreeable to you:

   [ ] 10% from Gross Receipts realized from sales

   [ ] 33% from Net Receiptsrealized from sales

Below are the wheeling specifications you provided to Robert (cross out or fill-in):

1. Type of System		
	[ ] Basic System	[ ] Group System
	[ ] 1 Key Number	[ ] Pairs
	[ ] 2 Key Number	[ ] Giants
	[ ] 3 Key Number	[ ] Conditional CS
	[ ] Six-Group	[ ] Positional
		[ ] Syst. w/Pivots

2. Amount of Numbers to be Wheeled ....

3. Prize Guarantee ....

4. Maximum Amount of Games ....

Fill in your address below and return this card to the address above:

Name _____	Phone _____
Street _____	The Best Time To Reach You
CitySt/Zip _____	_____

ONE TO WON   (Lottery Systems Consultants)

✉ | ONE TO WON
P.O.BOX 336 • Bowling Green Station
New York • NY 10274

☎ | 914-986-6518

☞ Expert Lottery Consultants for over 8 years and developers of 26 proven winning systems for Lotto, Pick-3, and Pick-4. ONE TO WON operates the most successful number clubs and hotline service in the U.S.A.

ONE TO WON received favorable reviews from the N.Y. Times as "...one of the leading prognosticators of Lotto." This company has helped thousands of players across the nation to win and obtain monetary rewards.

Two subsidiary companies—Happy Player and Keyhole—are also continually producing winning systems. They have written lottery columns for major lottery publications. Their systems are easy to understand and work well in all states. For only $2.00 (postage and handling), you can receive their winning system catalog, which includes:

• LOTTO CODE TAP	A Pick-6 Lotto System that has already produced many Jackpot winners ($19.95 + $2 p&h).
• SURROUND	Computer formulated boxes which contain the winners ($7.95 + $2 p&h)
• 4.S.EXTENSION	A remarkable Pick-3 chart system ($15.95 + $2 p&h)
• MERGER I	A Pick-3 chart system— 6 part system which gives you the winner each night ($29.95 + $2 p&h)
• KEYHOLE	A Pick-3 system—extraordinary accuracy ($39.95 + $2 p&h)

You can order directly using your credit cards by calling 1-914-986-6518 or order by mail from: *one to won systems* • P.O.Box 336 • Bowling Green Station • New York • NY 10274.

LOTTERY COLLECTORS SOCIETY

✉ | LOTTERY COLLECTORS SOCIETY
c/o Dave Parmalee • 1007 Luttrell Street
Knoxville • TN 37917

☎ | 615-577-6252
717-393-0843
201-543-6204

☞ **The Lottery Collectors Society** is a non-profit organization founded in 1988, dedicated to promoting the hobby of collecting used, void and sample lottery tickets and related advertising paraphenalia.

The club has members from more than 20 states. Members are interested in tickets for their beauty and relative scarcity. Trading between members is very active. Most trade ticket for ticket—there is practically no buying and selling among members. Most of the group's interest focuses on scratch-off instant games from around the country.

Membership dues are $10 for the first year. Benefits include a membership card and list, a monthly newsletter, new ticket lists and more. To join, or for more information and a sample newsletter, write to the society, c/o Dave Parmalee at the address above.

LOTTERY COMPUTER HARDWARE

✉	**LOTTERY COMPUTER SERVICES** Dept. of L.S.I. 2319 Calle Del Mundo Santa Clara • CA 95054	☎ 1-800-526-8899 1-408-980-1999 1-217-980-5149 (FAX)

LOTTERY COMPUTER SERVICES (L.C.S.) is offers complete IBM-Compatible computer systems at very competitive prices. Through a special arrangement with a direct importer of these high quality computer systems, L.C.S. can offer them to you at a considerably lower price than many retail computer stores.

These systems come complete with keyboard, monitor, and printer. And depending on your needs and budget there are four different configurations and prices available.

Basic Configuration to which a monitor and additional disk drives need to be added:
• "Turbo XT" Clone running at 10 megahertz (we can also provide more advanced systems, call for information)
• 512k memory*
• single 5.25" floppy drive
• MS-DOS (operating system) installed
• dot matrix printer

Here are the different *disk drive* and *monitor* configurations and their prices:

The *lowest* priced systems have Mono-Chrome (one color) Monitors: • MCDD=with an additional 5.25 floppy disk-drive$ 869.95 • MCHD=with a 20 megabyte internal hard-drive $1129.95	The *higher* priced system have high-quality color EGA Monitors: • CMDD=with an additional 5.25 floppy disk-drive$1429.95 • CMHD=with a 20 megabyte internal hard-drive $1669.95

To help you learn how to use your new computer a special program called "DOS Tutor" will be included with the system, so that the computer itself will show you how to use it right the first time. We will also include a free copy of the best selling book for beginning and intermediate computer users, "Using MS-DOS" published by Osborne/McGraw-Hill.

Complete Lotto Computer Systems

If you are a first-time computer owner, you'll appreciate our special software installation service: when you order a system with a hard-drive, L.C.S. will install the computer's operating system and the lottery software of your choice onto the drive. This sometimes intimidating process will be handled by trained technicians, so that when you receive your system you will simply plug it together, turn it on and begin computing to success.

LSI Publishing, Inc. offers the largest selection of lottery computer software programs found anywhere (see page, so you will be able to get the most from your computer; whether you want to see a complete statistical analysis of your favorite lottery game or you want to simply substitute your numbers into a large wheeling system and have the program check for winning tickets or everything inbetween.

There's software available for every type of lottery game (except for "Scratch-off" games, of course), and the best quality and largest selection of lottery software is available for IBM-compatibles. Because our computer systems come complete, there are no guesswork or hidden costs for those new to IBM-compatibles.

There is also a 90 day warranty on all computer parts and workmanship. If you have any questions regarding our Complete Lotto Computer Systems, call 1-800-526-8899 (inside CA 1-408-980-1999).

FLOTTO (IBM and compatibles)

✉ PC LIGHT INC.
P.O.Box 18532
Tampa • FL 33679-8532

☎ 1-813-837-3368

☞ FLOTTO™—Version 2.01—plays all Pick 5, 6 and 7 lotto games as well as Daily Pick-3 and Pick-4 games. Three ways to pick lottery numbers:
1. SUPERSPIN—the program will instantly generate a FLOTTO lottery ticket at the touch of a button.
2. SELECT MODE—a lottery ticket is created with the player's numbers and/or FLOTTO numbers.
3. WHEELER—wheel from 6 up to 12 numbers (player's and/or FLOTTO numbers).

WHAT CAN FLOTTO DO FOR YOU?

- There is no limit to the number of lottery games that may be played. Each player can have multiple files for every game. Files can hold from 1 to 1,000 lottery tickets.
- Complete error checking so you never duplicate a lottery ticket. Tickets can be reviewed, added or removed from a file at anytime.
- The program will automatically calculate each player's odds of winnings and instantly checks Winning Tickets in any file. A series of tones let you know when you have a winner.
- Printed listing of each file is available anytime.
- Works on a floppy or a hard drive. Instructions are "On-Line" self contained in the program. A separate routine is included that will automatically install FLOTTO onto your hard drive.
- FLOTTO works on all IBM and compatibles using DOS 2.0 and higher or UNIX V with vpix. Screen—color or monochrome (PC, XT, AT, PS2, LAPTOPS).

FLOTTO costs $24.95 plus $2 for shipping and handling. C.O.D. orders available.

LOTTO CHAMPION™ (IBM and compatibles)

✉ L.S.I. Publishing, Inc.
1259 El Camino Real
Menlo Park • CA 92540

☎ Call Toll-Free
1-800-526-8899 (outside CA)
1-408-980-1999 (in CA)

☞ LOTTO CHAMPION—a must for those that want to *Play With Control, Not Guesswork..* This sensational program for IBM and compatible computers was developed by European author G. Essl and it is packed with the best of Robert Serotic's wheeling systems.

LOTTO CHAMPION uses its powerful data-base system and the latest in AI Software Development. This program has nice screen color and easy to use "pull-down" menus for issuing commands. The unique backtracking system will take advantage not only of the **150 wheels** included in the package but will bring the Lottery History Base to life. The analysis menu offers three levels of detail, concluding with a comprehensive "advanced" report that covers almost any conceivable statistics.

Best of all, LOTTO CHAMPION has a lottery stimulator that lets you easily (and cheaply) experience the reality of playing the lottery over a long term. Just pick the numbers and wheel them into multiple combinations. Then, sit back and watch the program keep track over the simulated "years" of play, which can be done in a matter of hours.

WHAT CAN LOTTOCHAMPION DO FOR YOU?

This real champion among all lottery programs gives you instant access to multitudes of valuable information:

• **MULTIPLE DATA HISTORY BASES** • **ANALYSIS:** High-Low, Hot-Cold, Last Drawn, Average, Total Counts, Front-End, Odd-Even, Single-Multiple • **GRAPHS:** Frequency Chart, Hot&Cold Chart • **150 WHEELING SYSTEMS** (Full, Shortened, Key, Test Wheels).

Price: $59.95 plus s&h. The software is available on 3.5" and 51/4" floppy disks.

LONA (IBM and compatibles)

✉ LEADER SOFTWARE, INC.
P.O.Box 280 • Dept. 1480
Trenton • MI 48183

☎ TOLL-FREE
1-800-759-5662

☞ LONA™ — The LOttery Number Advisor

The lottery world was astounded with the recent announcement that certain lottery "number trends" actually outperformed random number selection by 30% and more. The discoveries were made by Professor Darrel A. Dolph. He is known across America as a lottery expert and columnist for several national magazines.

Professor Dolph's extensive research and development is now available in an amazing new computer software program called LONA™. The LOttery Number Advisor works with any IBM PC or compatible computer. It is extraordinarily simple to run.

WHAT CAN LONA™ DO FOR YOU?

This software gives you instant access to multitudes of valuable information:

• **Winning Number** histories • **RANGE** histories • **ADJACENCY** histories • **REPEAT** histories • **BALANCED GAME** histories • **LONGSHOT** histories

Besides these great features, there are graphs, charts, and Professor Dolph's newest innovation the **"MOVING AVERAGE FILTER."**

Man-months of hand calculations are completed in just seconds! With LONA™, you can perform virtually every lottery trend analysis imaginable... Price: $95.00 plus $5 (p&h). The software is available on 5¼ floppy disks. Also, ask about **BIG WHEEL™**!

LOTTO MASTER PROFESSIONAL (IBM&compatib.)

✉ JPM COMPUTER
P.O.Box 30742
Portland • OR 97230

☎ For More Information
503-287-8952

☞ LOTTO MASTER PROFESSIONAL (LMP) is a full-featured Lotto Management Program.

The program requires no statistical or higher math background from the user and is menu driven and easy to use without being simplistic. The screen displays are clear and logical and the explanations provided by the manual are easy to follow.

LMP can be used for any Pick-5 or Pick-6 Lotto game, and fully supports Bonus Number .

The program can create new games and is supplied with a utility to rebuild data, files in the event there are damaged or accidentaly erased.

WHAT CAN LOTTO MASTER PROFESSIONAL DO FOR YOU?

With Release 2, LMP offers a variety of powerful features:

• Maintains, tracks and checks **Bets** • Mantains a history of **Winning Numbers** • **Searches** and **Analyzes** history • **Generates Bets** through multiple built-in wheeling systems—both automatically and manually • Shows **Companion Numbers** for every number • Delivers detailed **Printed Reports** • Uses **"Quick Keys"** for rapid input!

One of many unique features is LMP's ability to isolate any period between two dates in the history file, and then to display, search and analyze that period for significant information! LMP is an all-purpose Lotto tool designed to aid in making decisions about placing bets and in tracking results. The program costs $49.95, including shipping and handling, and can be ordered directly from the above address. It will run on either hard drive or one or two floppies using color or B&W monitor.

PROBALOTO (IBM and compatibles)

✉ L.S.I. Publishing, Inc.
1259 El Camino Real
Menlo Park • CA 92540

☎ Call Toll-Free
1-800-526-8899 (outside CA)
1-408-980-1999 (in CA)

☞ PROBALOTO is menu driven. Probaloto (the probability lottery program) is used for selecting lottery numbers and numbers for other games of chance. You can choose numbers from a selected range to suit the requirements of the particular lottery. The numbers can be picked randomly (if desired), but the real power of the program is geared towards making weighted random selection. Lists of past drawings are entered into a data file (so-called HAT), then weighted and selected for your play. Probaloto also sorts the numbers selected.

PROBALOTO can select numbers for three types of lotto games—three numbers (zero to nine) for the Pick-3 game, four numbers (zero to nine) for the Pick-4 game and and also any state's regular lottery game(Pick-5, Pick-6, Pick-7, WIN 10). In addition there are several built-in wheeling systems offering partial wheeling from 8 to 30 numbers. You can also input any wheeling system you desire.

PROBALOTO gives the user desirable options for customizing number picks and the advantage of using full or shortened wheeling systems.

WHAT CAN PROBALOTO DO FOR YOU?

Probaloto is used for *selecting lottery numbers* and numbers for other games of chance.

Price: $39.95 plus s&h. The software is available on 51/4" floppy disks.

LET'S MAKE A WHEEL (IBM and compatibles)

✉ L.S.I. Publishing, Inc.
1259 El Camino Real
Menlo Park • CA 92540

☎ Call Toll-Free
1-800-526-8899 (outside CA)
1-408-980-1999 (in CA)

☞ LET'S MAKE A WHEEL (menu driven) is one of the most advanced wheeling programs on the market today. It will wheel all possible combinations to 59 numbers and wheel up to 100 numbers in abbreviated systems. It can be used with any lottery in any state because it can wheel lotteries with 5, 6, 7, 8, 9 and 10 numbers in each set (either 5/35 in Illinois, 6/49 in California, 7/11/80 in Pennsylvania, WIN 10 in New York, or casino KENO).

A wheel even has options to limit the output when wheeling all possible combinatons—you can limit the sets printed to a totals range. The program can learn any wheeling system you wish to use. The only limits are that the system must have less then 1,000 games (sets) and you can't wheel more than 100 numbers (the largest amount of numbers played in the U.S.A. is 80 in Pennsylvania's 7/11/80). This program is a great tool for any wheeling system player—it can read any type of wheel!

WHAT CAN LET'S MAKE A WHEEL DO FOR YOU?

LET'S MAKE A WHEEL is a great *wheeling program* offering Lotto Number Wheeling Systems for any Lotto game in the U.S.A., Canada, Australia and Europe. It can remember any custom made wheel and also computer generated systems offered by Robert Serotic's Custom Wheel Network. This program is also good for other games of chance.

Price: $39.95 plus s&h. The software is available on 51/4" floppy disks.

LOTTERY DOLLARS™ (IBM and compatibles)

✉	L.S.I. Publishing, Inc. 1259 El Camino Real • Suite 217 Menlo Park • CA 92540	☎	Call Toll-Free 1-800-526-8899 (outside CA) 1-408-980-1999 (in CA)

☞ **LOTTERY DOLLARS™ — I.2 version**

This excellent software was developed by Robert Serotic and Dr. Ronald Hoard (from Livermore Labs). It utilizes Serotic's powerful "Tables of Winning" and "Probability of Winning" so that your game numbers can be analyzed, balanced, and combined into the best system for your budget. Input any Basic system for a complete analysis and generation of "Tables of Winning.".

LOTTERY DOLLARS™ is a host of over 60 Basic systems and gives a wide selection from which to choose. Will also generate Full Systems from 7 to 22 numbers. It also has the ability to have other types of wheeling systems (such as those found in Robert's books) inputted into the program for substitution and printing of the system. Future *Lottery Dollars*™ disks will offer Key, Group and other types of systems and analysis.

WHAT CAN LOTTERY DOLLARS™ DO FOR YOU?

LOTTERY DOLLARS™ is the most powerful lotto wheeling system program with a unique feature—*WINNING TABLES*.. This excellent lottery program gives you instant access to multitudes of valuable information:

WHEELS player's numbers into system • Defines the **WINNING CONDITIONS** of systems in % • Develops "**PROBABILITY OF WINNING**" and odds for each wheeling system • **ANALYZE** and **BALANCE** player's numbers • **PRINTS-OUT** the substituted system • Allows to **INSTALL** any number of wheeling systems

Price: $39.95 plus s&h. It can be used for any Pick-6 Lotto and also for other games of chance and is available on 51/4" floppy disks.

LOTTO PRO PLUS™ (IBM and compatibles)

✉	L.S.I. Publishing, Inc. 1259 El Camino Real • Suite 217 Menlo Park • CA 92540	☎	Call Toll-Free 1-800-526-8899 (outside CA) 1-408-980-1999 (in CA)

☞ Computer Shopper: *"LottoPro+™ uses elaborate number crunching to predict probable future numbers."* Strong statistical Lottery package with Wheeling capabilities!

WHAT CAN LOTTO PRO+ DO FOR YOU?

- comes with a substantial database of past Lotto numbers drawn in CA and WA. Can keep data on unlimited lotteries;
- allows for auto-checking of tickets and uses total average filtering on number combinations; fast and easy to use menu bars similar to Lotus 1-2-3;
- develops 3 major charts — Draw/Miss graph, frequency chart, and comprehensive statistical chart;
- comes with section for Cash 3 and Cash 4;
- 7 different methods to develop probability charts which enable the user to evaluate numbers based on past performance. The most probable numbers can be used in any of the 57 abbreviated Basic systems.

LOTTO PRO+™ is good for any Pick-3&4, Pick-5, Pick-6, Pick-7, Pick-11 Lotto & Keno.

Price: $79.95 plus s&h. LottoPro+ is available on 3.5"MFD and 51/4 floppy disks (both IBM).

LOTTO PRO™   (Macintosh, IBM and compatibles)

✉ L.S.I. Publishing, Inc.
1259 El Camino Real • Suite 217
Menlo Park • CA 92540

☎ Call Toll-Free
1-800-526-8899 (outside CA)
1-408-980-1999 (in CA)

☞ **LOTTO PRO**™ offers the features of LOTTO PRO+ with the exception of the Pick-3 and Pick-4 section. Has complete statistical and wheeling capabilities. is good for any Pick-6, Pick-7, Pick-11 Lotto & Keno. Available on 3.5"MFD(IBM and Macintosh) and 51/4" floppy disk (IBM).   Price: $79.95 plus s&h.

LOTTERY BOSS PACK   (IBM&comp. • Apple • Commodore)

✉ L.S.I. Publishing, Inc.
1259 El Camino Real
Menlo Park • CA 92540

☎ Call Toll-Free
1-800-526-8899 (outside CA)
1-408-980-1999 (in CA)

☞ This combined package of all six Lottery Boss Singles was called "one of the most complete Lotto programs on the market" by L.S. Love, editor of *The Lotto Edge*. Keep in mind that you need the Key disk, **Lottery Boss III**, to use the remaining disks.

Lottery Boss III™   *Key Disk* (menu driven)—needed to run any of the disks listed below! Operates as the main data base entry point for storing past winning numbers for all types of lotto number games (Pick-3, 4, 5, 6, 7, and 11) on which the other disks can access information. It creates data disks, works one set at a time for unlimited data usage. All information entered can be edited. "Tally Boards" are created from inputted data. Random number generation is available from a variety of sources; from 100% Random and Selected Elimination, to fun number generators such as lottery horoscopes and slot machines.   Price: $24.95 + s&h

Report Master™   (requires key disk Lottery Boss III)
Generates statistical and analytical reports for both Lotto games and Pick-3/4, Cycle-Graph report, Ranking report, Past Probability report, Power Ratings report, Occurence report, and a Complete Lotto History report. For Pick-3/4 you can generate a Compiled or Selected Best Box report, Position Chart, Selected History or Complete History report, and a Single Set Search. All reports may be sent to either the screen or the printer.   Price: $24.95 + s&h

Pick Master™   (requires key disk Lottery Boss III)
Offers an alternative to using Lotto Number Systems. Players of Lotto 6/7 may create their own "sets" of numbers using the data in Lottery Boss III™ and arranges it in order of occurrence to make your field. In order to create the best field of numbers from which to choose, Pick Master will provide for each digit; a % Bracket, a Top/Bottom Bracket, a Roll Over Factor, and a Power Rating. You can also Discard and Back Out digits. You can then print out a variety of additional information and save your sets to disk.   Price: $24.95 + s&h

Lotto Analyzer™   (requires key disk Lottery Boss III)
Creates a variety of statistical and analytical reports, Lotto Frequency Ratio's Analysis (number frequency), a Lotto Number Compatibility Analysis (digit forcaster), a Lotto Successive Digit Analyzer, and a Lotto Sectional Frequency Analysis. Also—calculates Odds, provides a Lotto Winning Set Locater and a Pick 6/7 Set Eliminator.   Price: $24.95 + s&h

Lottery Wheeler™   (requires key disk Lottery Boss III)
Comes with 72 Wheeling Systems. Other wheels (such as those found in Robert Serotic's books) can be inputed into the program and used fully. Allows you to choose a System, input your numbers, and have them substituted into the System and the complete games will be printed out. (check for winning games by using the Winning Set Locator on Lotto Analyzer™). Also includes Boxers for Pick 3/4. Easy to use.   Price: $24.95 + s&h

Lotto Eliminator™   (requires key disk Lottery Boss III)
A combination of statistical features and tools for Pick Master—Skip and Hit Chart, Skip Group Totals Chart, Odd and Even Analysis, Bell Curve Set Totals Analyzer and Bell Curve Grapher, Odd and Even Eliminator, Bell Curve Eliminator, and Your Picks v.s. Lotto Winners Search. Also includes a special section of highly useful Lottery Player's Supplies which will print out graph paper (2 sizes), data entry sheets, track record sheets, ruled line sheets and dotted line (chart) paper.   Price: $24.95 + s&h

Serotic's LOTTERY HOTLINE—Direct (U.S.A)

✉ LOTTERY HOTLINE—Direct
65 Washington — Suite 141
Santa Clara • CA 95050

☎ 1-408-980-5174
FREE Consultation
Services

☞ LOTTERY HOTLINE—Direct is the first live lottery hotline in the world!
The huge volume of letters Robert Serotic has been receiving has surpassed his ability to reply, so unfortunatelly not all questions can be answered in writing. Many players ask for help or advice that is very important in improving their chances of winning. In order to help players accomplish their dreams, on August 1st, 1988 Robert opened a direct "Lottery Hotline" where you can call and obtain your information right away. "Robert's Lottery Hotline—Direct" is open every Wednesday from 3 p.m.-7 p.m. Pacific Time. Before you call, make sure that you know what you want to ask since every caller can discuss his/her matter!!. Don't forget that many players will be waiting to get through, so let your friends get the winning edge, too!

CAN YOU OBTAIN A "SURE TIP" BY CALLING 1-408-980-5174?

The service does not offer winning numbers, nor predict future drawings. The main goal of Robert's Hotline is to help those players using wheeling systems. Here are some of the most important questions that every player needs to learn about::

• Selection of a Wheeling System • Selection of numbers for different types of wheels • Balancing the number selection • Modifying Pick-6 Wheeling Systems into the Pick 5 or Pick 7 Wheels • Custom Wheel Network • Computer Generated Systems Network • Optimal selection of computer software • Statistical charts • Lotto budget and financial plan • How to avoid gambling

You can call every Wednesday, 3 p.m.-7 p.m. Pacific Time

Lottery Players of America LOTTERY HOTLINE (U.S.A)

✉ LPA Lottery Hotline
1255 W. Broad Street
Stratford • CT 06497

☎ 1-900-370-5112
Hotline available from
touchtone phones

☞ A "900" audiotex phone service that provides up-to-the-minute results for each and every state lottery game:
• Daily numbers • Lotto • Keno...and every state lottery game.
The service also offers the results for all Canadian and Australian lotto games.

SPECIAL SERVICES

The service updates results within an hour of their official announcement

24 hours a day
7 days a week

The cost of the phone call appears on the caller's phone bill and will be $.75 for the first minute, $.50 for each additional minute.

DISCOUNT OFFERS

Also available on the line are special discount offers to join several clubs, or to play the lotteries in the U.S. and Canada. Jackpot values for upcoming lotto drawings for each state are available for selection as well as the opportunity to order entries for several of the big Jackpot lotteries.

Callers can also access with the same phone call a service that picks personal lucky numbers at random for any lottery.

LOTTERY ON-LINE   (Computer Data Base Services)

✉ Lottery On-Line Services, Inc.
P.O.BOX 13103 • Station
El Paso • TX 79913

☎ Information: 915-581-0344
FREE info. by MODEM: 915-833-7030

☞ **Lottery On-Line Services** offer WORLDWIDE lottery data base access with the ability to download lottery data bases to the Entertainment On-Line, Inc. TRACKER and WHEELER program disk so you can analyze and play lottery games with the skill of an expert. You can now follow virtually every lottery game in the world.

WHY TO JOIN THIS UNIQUE SERVICE

It is extremely desirable for a lottery player to have immediate access to the very latest developments of the games throughout the world...plus the use of vital services that could help to make big winners.

These are some examples of the services offered:
• Complete up to date results of Lotteries around the world.
• Purchase of tickets for the lotteries worldwide and in the U.S.A.
• Wheeling Systems for any kind of Lotto number game.
• Programs for tracking and analyzing lottery numbers.
• Audiotapes to assist the Lottery player with selection of numbers.
• Communication with other subscribers to campare methods of play.

Subscribing to such a comprehensive Lottery Service could be even more rewarding as lottery games increase. With today high technology, it will permit you to paticipate in the Lotteries inteligently, resulting in a wider variety of valuable services and data to make selections a quicker and easier task.

LOTTO GENIE

✉ A.W. ENTERPRISES
4001 N. St. Joseph Ave.
Evansville • IN 47712

☎ 812-426-0853

☞ A.W. Enterprises markets a mechanical random number selector called the Lotto Genie®, which aids players in generating their own "Quick Picks." It is small enough to hold in the palm of the hand or carry in a pocket.

The Lotto Genie® is a short, canister-shaped device sealed shut with a clear lid that looks like an upside down funnel. A ring inside is drilled with a number of small, numbered holes—one to represent each number in a lotto field. A hollow compartment in the center holds five, six or seven small balls (depending on which game it was designed for). A plunger on the bottom of the canister is used to eject the balls, which then roll randomly into the holes in the numbered ring.

Lotto Genie® is available directly from A.W. Enterprises. The price for any type is $6 plus $2 for shipping and handling.

LOTTO GENIES are currently availeble for these types of games:

6/36	Massachusetts Delaware • Iowa D.C. • W. Virginia	5/40 5/40	Rhode Island Connecticut Maryland	6/45 6/46 6/48	Australia New Jersey Pennsylvania
5/35	Illinois		NY • Tri State	6/49	California • Florida
5/39	Florida	5/44	Michigan • Missouri	6/54	Illinois • NY
6/39	Arizona • Canada		Ohio • Washington		Lotto America

NLPA
(National Lottery Players Association)

NLPA Administrative Offices 701-I Devonshire Dr. Champaign • IL 61820	Telephone: 1-800-872-6572 (1-800-USA-NLPA) 1-217-352-3072 1-217-352-3073 (FAX)

Phillip A. Gillespie	*(President)*	*217-762-3521*	*Fax 217-762-9914*
Dale R. Ardvidson	*(Executive Director)*	*217-352-3072*	*Fax 217-352-3073*
Gordon L. Cohen	*(Managing Editor)*	*217-352-3072*	*Fax 217-352-3073*
Kristan Cockerill	*(Public Info. Director)*	*217-352-3072*	*Fax 217-352-3073*
Ken Miller	*(Print Shop Coordinator)*	*217-762-9725*	*Fax 217-762-9914*

The National Lottery Players Association, or NLPA, is a national consumer group for lottery players. Established in October 1988, NLPA publishes a comprehensive and timely reference guide to all U.S. state lotteries. The reference book, called the NLPA Handbook, provides information on how to play, the odds, statistics and a variety of other information of interest to lottery enthusiasts. It also includes a directory of all state lotteries as well as NLPA Associate Members, companies that provide services or supplies to lottery consumers.

NLPA Handbook

The NLPA Handbook is updated monthly to keep up with changes in the industry. Along with the monthly handbook updates, members receive a monthly newsletter that reports any late-breaking news. NLPA members are also entitled to a variety of consumer discounts on products and services from Associate Members and other businesses.

How to Join

- Lottery players may join NLPA by telephone or by mail.
- A one-year membership costs $39 plus $2.50 for shipping and handling of membership materials.
- Those who call the toll-free number, 1-800-872-6572 (1-800-USA-NLPA), may pay for their membership with Visa, MasterCard, Discover or American Express. Members may also join by mail and pay by credit card (include card number and expiration date), a personal check or a money order.
- Mail orders should be sent to the NLPA Administrative Offices at the above address.
- NLPA membership materials are usually shipped within 2 to 4 weeks after the order is received. Membership includes an unconditional 90-day money-back guarantee.

Robert Serotic and L.S.I. Publishing, Inc. thank the directors and public information officials of the state lotteries throughout the U.S. for information used in this book. This cooperation, however, does not constitute a sanction or endorsement of Robert Serotic and L.S.I. Publishing, Inc. by any state lottery commission.

NOTES